African Dance in Ghana: Contemporary Transformations

African Dance in Ghana: Contemporary Transformations

F Nii-Yartey

Professor of Dance Studies, University of Ghana, Legon

Foreword by **Emeritus Professor J H Kwabena Nketia**

Edited by Marian Horowitz and Andrews K Agyemfra-Tettey

mot juste

Published in 2016 by Mot Juste Limited
134 Riverside, Milk Yard, London E1W 3SY, United Kingdom
www.motjuste.co.uk

Cover photograph by Karla Hoffman
All photographs are by the author, unless credited otherwise
Illustrations by David Akushe Amoo

British Library Cataloguing in Publication Data. A catalogue record for
this book is available from the British Library

African Dance in Ghana: Contemporary Transformations
www.africandanceinghana.com

Includes bibliographical references and index

ISBN 978-0-9569670-2-2

Printed by KOPA, Lithuania

To all my children
and to the memory of my parents:
Nii 'Kojo-fio' Tackie (Taatse) and Naa Afie Quao (Taanye)

and to my artistic fathers:
Professor Emeritus Albert Mawere-Opoku
Professor Emeritus J H Kwabena Nketia

Contents

African Dance in Ghana: Contemporary Transformations

Foreword

by J H Kwabena Nketia, Emeritus Professor

It is a great joy and a pleasure to endorse this exposition of contemporary transformations of African dance forms in Ghana by Professor Francis Nii-Yartey, a veteran choreographer who has contributed immensely to the development of the Dance Theatre in Ghana. I thoroughly enjoyed reading it and recommend it highly not only to students of the performing arts of Africa and its diaspora but also to the general public.

Although Nii did not tell me precisely why he particularly wanted me to write this foreword, I assumed that he would like me to throw some light on the formative period of the dance-theatre which followed the period of cultural awakening that gained momentum shortly after the proclamation of independence, for the struggle for independence from colonial rule in the 1950s was not only a struggle for political freedom and national development but also a struggle for cultural freedom and the assertion of consciousness of cultural identity.

This way of looking at the independent status of Ghana reflected the thinking, creative imagination and modes of expression of artists, musicians and writers who responded inwardly to President Nkrumah as he yelled "Free at Last!" on the eve of Independence Day. It moulded the orientation of those of us who were invited to participate in the planning and implementation of the protocols of the State Functions Secretariat of the First Republic and its successors. Freedom meant not only political and cultural freedom, but also creative freedom — including the freedom to adopt, adapt or re-create traditional materials in contemporary contexts, always ensuring that all practices in both traditional and contemporary contexts — and not only customary practices, as the 1992 constitution stipulates — that "dehumanise or are injurious to the physical and mental wellbeing of a person are prohibited".

I was deeply involved in the pursuit of this creative freedom and its rationale and contexts of application in my capacity as Deputy Director of the Institute of African Studies when it began at the request of the government of the Republic of Ghana, and the early phase of its development which began with the appointment of Professor Albert Mawere-Opoku as the Artistic Director of the Ghana Dance Ensemble, a position he relinquished when Francis Nii-Yartey, a member of the first batch of dance students groomed by him, was ready in our opinion to take over from him.

What was noteworthy about this development was the fact that the initiative came from the government of the Republic and not from the university, which had just emerged from its tutelage as a University College of the University of London. Except for the few students from the colonial era who grumbled about the invasion of the hallowed precincts of the university campus by 'Dondology', the innovation was uneventful, partly because of the fact that the academic integrity of African Studies as a field of scholarship had been amply demonstrated in the Department of Sociology where I held the position of Research Fellow and developed studies and source materials in African Music and Related Arts.

However my 'extracurricular' activities were not boisterous! Moreover, although a member of the academic community, I did not confine myself to the university campus. I was also an active member of the Interim Committee for an Arts Council of Ghana, as well as the statutory Arts Council when it was established. In addition I also participated in the work of the State Functions Secretariat's activities that validated the assumption that setting up a National Dance Company – and along with it a School of Music, Dance and Drama in Legon in the 1960s under the auspices of the Institute of African Studies – would not only be a landmark but a valuable means of promoting an African cultural renaissance on campus.

Although my active participation in national events and the evidence of my scholarly output also contributed in part to the decision to set up the Ghana Dance Ensemble at the university, it was the thrust of

Dr Nkrumah's ideology of promoting 'the African Personality' that paved the way for this and related institutional developments on campus. Establishing an African university unencumbered intellectually by the goals and values of our colonial past was perhaps Nkrumah's greatest academic ambition and so he was generous with funding for research and development and also ensured that the Institute had semi autonomy in the early stages of its development as a centre for the cultures of Africa and its diaspora.

As a result of this initiative, which worked out well as various lines of collaboration with relevant departments were developed, the University of Ghana saw itself at the peak of this development as a centre for the creative arts – a development we shared with participants in the Commonwealth Universities' Conference held in Edinburgh, and which prompted the University of Ghana, Legon, to challenge any attempt to relocate any of its components elsewhere outside the university campus. The modest Ghana Dance Ensemble, which had metamorphosed on campus into a National Dance Theatre company under the directorship of *war* Francis Nii–Yartey, had become so well established that getting the University to agree to its relocation in the new National Theatre in Accra became a tug of war, something that could have been settled amicably by recognising the complementary roles and functions of the two organisations. Maintaining a repertoire dance company outside the university in a National Theatre, designed for this and other productions for the general public, should not have been confused with the academic objectives of a university that ensures not only that its academic community has access to the performing arts but also that it contributes to its growth and development through research and its application to specific issues in the national context.

The artistic freedom that was unleashed by Independence and the opportunities of developing new lines of artistic collaboration across Africa and beyond led to the stabilisation and general acceptance of the modest transformation described above. This was spearheaded by Albert Mawere-Opoku, the first Artistic Director, whose modest creative development in choreographic terms was picked up by Professor Nii-Yartey, his able successor. He greatly elaborated on this foundation as he created more dynamic works that told their own stories and presented historical and contemporary problems to appreciative audiences not only in Ghana, but also elsewhere in Africa and other parts of the world.

It is this development, which is Professor Nii-Yartey's unique contribution to African dance theatre, that he has taken pains to outline and develop in this book so that students of the performing arts of Africa, who need to be familiar with this ongoing historical process and its antecedents, can appreciate how ethnographic facts and expressions become creative resources and artistic expressions in the perception of the artist who presents these in new contexts of application in a manner that enables the performer to interpret it in his movements. Naturally the theatre goer in turn learns to appreciate not only the rich diversity that the traditional sources provide but also what Nkrumah envisaged would be the unique contribution of the arts, and dance in particular to culture and nation building. *saying there are a lot of diff types of ppl & now everyone can learn other ppls culture*

For example, since cultural action and processes are guided or shaped by the concepts and values held by a people, after the Declaration of Independence President Nkrumah reiterated now and then that national values that supersede ethnic and sectional values should be articulated at the earliest opportunity and enforced within the integrative process of nation building through the arts and appropriate directives.

Because the practice of embodying such directives in a national cultural policy document was not a regular course of action until it was established at an inter-governmental conference of UNESCO in the 1960s, a blueprint for such a cultural policy for independent Ghana did not exist. And so President Nkrumah embodied these in his public speeches and writings, such as his autobiography in which he takes pains to stress the importance of overcoming cultural chauvinism in independent Africa. Addressing his countrymen in particular, he stresses that

"in the higher reaches of our national life, there should be no reference to Fantes, Ashantis, Ewes, Gas, Dagombas, strangers and so forth, but we call ourselves

Ghanaians – all brothers and sisters, members of the same community. For until we ourselves purge from our own minds this tribal chauvinism and prejudice of one against the other, we shall not be able to cultivate the wider spirit of brotherhood which our objective of Pan Africanism calls for." (1961:168)

In other words, national integration in Ghana was not only an internal political priority as far as he was concerned, but also a necessary prelude and foundation for a wider Pan-Africanism which calls for affinities beyond ethnicity and nation. That is why what seemed pertinent at Independence above everything else was not the strengthening of ethnicity – the rationale of indirect rule in the colonial period – but a new sense of nationhood, which had to be nurtured not only through such policy statements but preferably also through cultural action and relevant institutions that transcend ethnic boundaries.

hold e/o hard in hand / dont just associate w ur group ot pp!

On the same basis, in the higher reaches of our national life, 'ethnic traditions' – particularly specific items of contemporary relevance such as artefacts, music and dance forms, etc. – become items of a 'national' legacy, not by legislation but by metamorphosis. What belongs on a lower level to a community or an ethnic group, which merits similar redefinition and adoption, automatically becomes national on a higher level of application. It is because of such transformational possibilities that such processes provided that culture was viewed as a tool for the promotion of the new sense of nationhood. However, as President Nkrumah again put it, the challenge of independence went beyond a return to the past:

"We have to work hard to evolve new patterns, new social customs, new attitudes to life, so that while we seek the material, cultural and economic advancement of our country, while we raise her standards of life, we shall not sacrifice their fundamental happiness." (1957:169)

He defines this happiness as:

"The gifts of laughter and joy, a love of music, a lack of malice, and absence of the desire for vengeance for our wrongs, all things of intrinsic worth in a world sick of injustice, revenge, fear and want... These are the values we must not sacrifice unheedingly in pursuit of material progress. That is why we say that self-

government is not an end in itself." (1957:169)

Following his view of the sort of 'fundamental happiness' he hoped would be maintained in independent Ghana, now and then he also mentioned specific projects that could fall within a blueprint for a national cultural policy. After announcing in his second development plan that "we intend to examine carefully the possibilities of building up a tourist industry," he states:

"I hope very much that we can build a National Cultural Centre where our own

musicians and singers, and artists of international repute can perform."

(1961:121)

A national theatre movement, sustained and guided by our values and propelled by new directions of creativity, would be a dynamic asset for the promotion of this 'fundamental happiness' in contemporary contexts if it was inclusive, transformative and multi-ethnic in its orientation, and also creates space for both contextualisation and creative innovations.

That is why at the inauguration of the *Osagyefo Players*, his own presidential drama group at which I happened to be present, he expanded on the rationale behind this personal initiative he had taken to augment the ongoing thrust in re-organising and promoting culture in contemporary contexts. He reminded the gathering that:

"We have in Ghana and in Africa a rich cultural heritage in art, music, drama,

paintings and sculpture, which colonialism sought in vain to destroy. Our culture

and traditions have survived because they possess a special in-born power, a

peculiar cultural image, which we must now take upon ourselves to cultivate and

develop. What we are about to set up now— and that is why we are here— must

therefore rest in a healthy and dynamic expression of African genius and creative

power. African art and ethos are bound up with the forms of our social and

cultural development."

He then continues to list other areas of culture and development that he had initiated:

"As you know, I have initiated the establishment of the Institute of Art and Culture, the Institute of African Studies and the School of Music Dance and Drama at Legon. We hope to launch a Film and Television School for training of producers and artistes. We already have a Ghana Symphony Orchestra and a Choir, which are showing great promise. All these institutions and this drama group, which we are initiating today, mark a forward step in the development of the arts in Ghana."

Principles of Cultural Action

The above principles which I have abstracted from President Nkrumah's speeches and elaborated from my personal understanding and interpretation of their significance in various contexts of application, have continued to be valid since their declaration in the immediate post-Independence era, even though we still have a long way to go in their implementation. For example, although we have made reasonable progress in the fields of choral music and commercial entertainment music, we cannot yet boast of the kind of vigorous concert life President Nkrumah had experienced in his long sojourn abroad and which he envisaged could be emulated in Ghana. Hence his brief reference to artists of international repute is similarly noteworthy, for while he was an ardent nationalist and strongly supported our indigenous expressive forms, he was also interested in their creative extensions. Accordingly he was accommodating and believed in the growth and development that can emerge from fruitful cultural exchange as well as the coexistence of cultures as areas of state policy initiative.

It was because of this and his ardent commitment to Pan-Africanism that he suggested that an evening concert be included in the official programme of the celebration of the First Republic, and that Philipa Schuyler, the African-American composer-performer whom he knew during his student days in the US, be invited as a special guest for this auspicious state occasion. The first half of the programme consisted of choral works by Ephraim Amu, Isaac Riverson and myself, while the second half consisted of my *Republic Suite* (in seven movements played by Charles Simmons (flute) and myself (piano), and the piano works of the guest artist, Philipa Schuyler, played by herself.

While promoting contemporary creativity, the models of excellence in our traditional culture, and their effective use or transformations in contemporary contexts, were never overlooked. For example, although President Nkrumah was not a traditional Paramount Chief before he assumed office as President of the Republic of Ghana, he became one on an even higher level by metamorphosis as I made the *atumpan* drums play his appellations, attributing to him the deeds and qualities of our great kings of yore.

Similarly royal traditional ensembles heralded his presence as he stood or walked across the carpet, something he recalls with great appreciation and admiration in his autobiography (1961:238) as perhaps "the most colourful and impressive of all. This was the State Opening of Parliament on 4 July." He continues:

> "My arrival at Parliament House was heralded by the beating of traditional drums and the cheers of watching Ghanaians. A 21-Gun Salute was fired by a troop of the Ghana Reconnaissance Squadron, after which I inspected the Guard of Honour formed by the Third Battalion of the Ghana Regiment with the President's Colour and the Army Band. I was then escorted to the House in a procession led by the State Sword Bearers and including the Mace Bearer and eight Linguists drawn from many parts of the country, State Horns – *mmenson* – were sounded by the Juaben State Ntahera. I then took my seat on the Presidential Throne, carved in the form of a stool adorned with golden traditional stool symbols."

Naturally it was the 'African touch' in the ceremony that impressed him most, for it took him, and indeed the entire assembly and the cheering crowds by surprise. It made an impact in its own way on this occasion on the ongoing process of national awakening and reconstruction, while the 21-Gun Salute and Inspection of the Guard of Honour, formerly the act of the Colonial Governor, showed that politically we had taken over the reins of government, and would use the same army commanded by Ghanaian generals to defend our land. Political freedom meant not only cultural freedom but the freedom to adopt, adapt or re-create foreign materials for application in contemporary contexts, a position that enables us to deal with the challenges of inter-culturalism in music and related arts without losing tract of the traditional African foundations of one's creativity.

I believe that this in essence represents the rationale behind not only the creative of work of Francis Nii-Yartey but also his concept of the nature and scope of the training programmes in African dance forms that should be developed to sustain and expand what has been achieved thus far. That is why I have continued to stand by him as he developed the *Noyam Phase* of his dream for the growth and development of a contemporary African dance culture in Ghana that exemplifies our own African sense of modernity.

J H Kwabena Nketia, Emeritus Professor (left) with F Nii-Yartey

Acknowledgements

Words are insufficient to express the gratitude I owe to my teachers, inspirers and role models: the Emeritus Professor Mawere-Opoku and Emeritus Professor J H Kwabena Nketia for the special interest they showed in my professional career and providing me with the opportunity to direct the Ghana Dance Ensemble.

My profound and sincere thanks go to my students, dancers and collaborators, and the following colleagues whose friendship and support, spanning over three decades, encouraged me to "keep on keeping on": Grace Djabatey-Laing, David Akushe Amoo, Daniel Nii Addokwei Moffatt, Korkor Amerteifio, Oh! Nii Kwei Sowah, Dr. Bob Ramdhanie, 'H' Patten, Professor Sharon Friedler, Professor Kariamu Welsh, Germaine Acogny and Helmut Vogt, Jeannine Osayande, Monty Thompson and Arnold Sobers.

My unqualified gratitude goes to Professor Kofi Anyidoho and Dr Patrick Awuah for their friendship and support, and who, following in the steps of pioneers like Dr Ephraim Amu, Albert Mawere-Opoku and Emeritus Professor J H Kwabena Nketia, Efua Sutherland and others, took it upon themselves to ensure that the university community in Ghana understands and appreciates the value of the performing arts in academia. To Dr Ben Abdallah I say thank you for all the opportunities you provided to help dance to grow in this country.

I am deeply grateful to the many critics and journalists who made it their business to capture some essence of my choreography and development of dance in this country: Enimil Ashong, formerly of the *Weekly Spectator* and the *Ghanaian Times*, who literally followed my work in his writings, from the 1970s to date; and from whom I received a lot of insight into my own work – and I hasten to say to some of the most scathing criticism on my artistic journey. I would also like to mention Nana Benyin Dadson of the *Mirror* and *Showbiz*, Addowkei Moffatt, Nii

Korley Laryea, John Owoo, Paa Kayper Mensah, Nat Nunoo Amarteifio and a host of writers who helped to guide my creative impulses on to the right path.

To the numerous promoters of my works: Olaf Henson, Dr Bob Ramdhanie, Jan Drissen, Erwin Schellekens, Jaques Van Meel and others, I say "many thanks" for believing in my creative works.

My special thanks also go to Jo Butterworth and Liesbeth Wildschut who edited sections of the materials which appeared in their book, Jo Butterworth and Liesbeth Wildschut, *Contemporary Choreography – A Critical Reader (2009), London and New York: Routledge.*

I register my profound appreciation to Rex Danquah, the man who created the opportunity for me to choreograph the opening and closing ceremonies for almost all the major sporting events hosted by Ghana, therefore helping to marry sports and the arts in a significant way in the country. I respect your vision and calmness.

To my great friends, Professor Richard Douglass and Marian Horowitz for their unflinching support during the process of putting this book together. To Marian, I am greatly indebted to you, for the superb and meticulous manner in which you edited the manuscript, and for getting it ready for publishing. I greatly appreciate the open mindedness with which you relate to me and others as well. Many thanks.

To my former secretaries, Juliana Hanson, Felicia Asampana and Peace Parku, my appreciation for your patience, kindness and care in handling the typing of the rough manuscript over the years. To Fati Tunteya, thank you for sharing your knowledge of Dagomba culture with me. To Samuel S Obodai for the work on the dance map.

My unqualified appreciation goes to Andrews K Agyemfra-Tettey, who in spite of persistent power outages, stayed up late in the night to process photographs and to organise the pages in this book.

Finally, to my children and my entire immediate and extended family, for putting up with me all these years as I share quality time and resources meant for them, with my numerous professional engagements. The show, as they say, must go on.

F Nii-Yartey
University of Ghana, Legon

December 10, 2012

African Dance in Ghana: Contemporary Transformations

Introduction

My objective in this book is to shed some light on the nature and significance of traditional dances as well as the emerging contemporary African dance expression in Ghana. I have therefore set myself the difficult task of dealing with an art form that is essentially transient.

The materials discussed here have been made possible by my own observations and work carried out by my predecessors, as well as historical and cultural materials made available to me during my research work spanning many years.

I do hope that not only students of dance will understand and appreciate the contents of this work, but that the general public will also enjoy reading this as basic source material on aspects of the rich dance traditions of Ghana.

F Nii-Yartey
University of Ghana, Legon

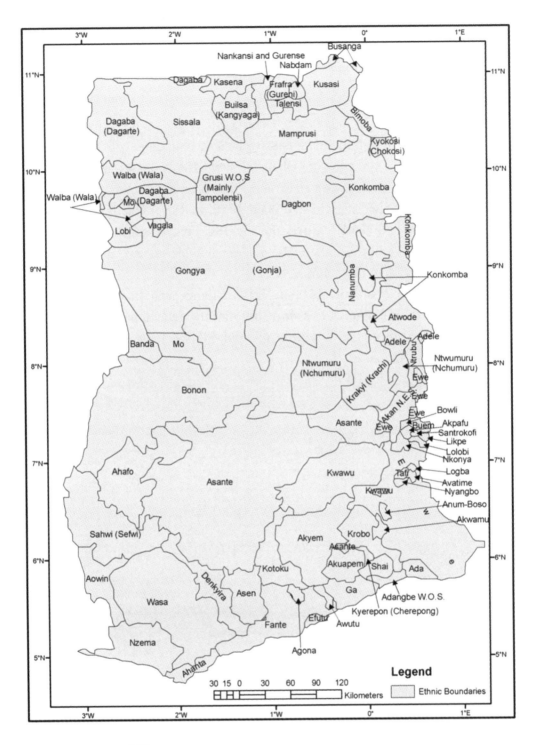

Ethnic map of Ghana

African Dance in Ghana: Contemporary Transformations

CHAPTER 1

The People of Ghana

Ghana, with a total land mass of 235,000 square kilometres and a population heading to 26 million people has, like many of her other African cousins, several linguistic and cultural groupings. The Ewe people occupy the south-eastern corner of the country. The Frafra and others occupy the northern sector, while the Nzema are located in the south-western part of Ghana. The Brong (Bonon), Ahafo and Ashanti are in the middle belt, while the Fante and Ga-Damgbe (Ga, Adangbe and Shai) occupy the south. This multi-lingual structure, however, may be grouped into two main cultures:

- the northern culture – with its Sudanic flavour – well adapted and fused with the indigenous culture of the people. This blend makes the culture of this vast savannah region inhabited by the Dagomba (Dagbon), Lobi, Moshie (in what is now Burkina Faso), Frafra, Dagarte and others unique in many respects
- the southern culture – characterised by comparatively greener vegetation and dominated by Akan, Ewe, Ga-Damgbe, Fante, Nzema and Guan-speaking people.

The vegetation and ecology of these two areas have had considerable effect on the occupation, vocation and cultural activities of the inhabitants. In the northern sector, the main occupation of the people is the growing of rice, yam, millet and the production of shea-butter and leather works. The lush vegetation of the south, coupled with the fact that most of the political and commercial activities of the country are centred there, so far enjoys many more occupational and vocational opportunities than the northern sector.

During the colonial period which lasted until 1957, when the country was known as the Gold Coast, attempts were made by the then British colonial government and foreign missionaries to discourage the cultural practices of the people. Western cultural values were highly encouraged. As a result, large numbers of people were lured out of the rural areas where the practice of traditional arts was much more significant, to seek clerical appointments and other jobs in the cities of the south. Some of the artists amongst them abandoned their arts in favour of new and 'foreign' skills to enable them survive the treacherous city life. This situation adversely affected many of the cultural practices in the country during the period.

It was therefore not surprising when soon after independence, the first President of Ghana, Dr Kwame Nkrumah, himself a man of culture and a committed Pan-Africanist, saw the potential of the arts in the development process of the new nation. He approved the establishment of an Institute of African Studies at the University of Ghana and the Institute of Arts and Culture in Accra and gave them generous support to enable these institutions to spearhead the restoration and development of African arts and culture in general. The following account, especially the new developments in dance, form part of this vision.

The old building, Institute of African Studies, University of Ghana, Legon

CHAPTER 2

Traditional Dance: an Introduction

Many African communities generally regard dance and other forms of artistic and cultural expression as important components of life's events. Therefore, traditional belief systems, concepts of birth, education, religion, politics, economics, death and other social activities manifest their importance to some degree in such artistic forms as dance, music, poetry and the arts. Dance, as a non-verbal communication tool, is one of the most powerful symbols and social indicators in African tradition. This book discusses the significance and development of dance in Africa, with special emphasis on Ghanaian traditions and the changes that have occurred in recent times.

Body Posture in Ghanaian Dance

The basic cultural values and aesthetic qualities of dance include the notion of beauty in body posture. This is conceptualised in terms of 'curves' and other circular images in almost all the traditional dance forms of Ghana. The body is almost always slightly rounded, the knees relaxed, while the weight of the movement is earth-bound. The belief is that circular images give a sense of perpetual motion and completeness of being. A good dancer is therefore expected to perform with an inner sense of roundness and balance. This aesthetic notion, in many cases, runs counter to the linear and angular body stance maintained in some non-African dance forms like ballet and the *Flamenco*, for example. In these two dances, beauty of body alignment and technical perfection seem to be the overriding factor.

Dance and other artistic forms can bring about meaningful relationships, mutual respect and a sense of belonging among members of the community. They also serve as indexes to the values and structures that enable the community to express and interpret the various events of life. When, for example, a Ghanaian priestess (who serves as an intermediary between the unseen world and the community) dances, her facial expressions, gestures, the dynamic qualities of her movements and use of space help determine the characteristics of the spiritual entity she represents. The practice of these values as community experience provides necessary links to others based on kinship, religion, common language and world view of the people. As noted by Mawere-Opoku:

> "...we, the people, accept the dancer's role as the centre of our lives – in his subtle flexion of hands and fingers, our prayers; in his thrusting arms – our thanksgiving; in his stamp and pause – our indignation; in his leap and turns – our frivolity – our defiance; in his bow – our allegiance; his halting steps – our reverence. Thus he dances, not alone but with us and we with him. We are not spectators, but co-creators and participants in the dramas of the African way of life. Many communities in Ghana believe in and cherish the gift and efficacy of this philosophy."

To create and sustain dance depends on the ability of its creators to arouse and inspire emotional involvement – based on the community's knowledge of the aesthetic and symbolic significance of the dances. Social, religious and other needs often help to create these dances. However, historical, ecological, environmental, climatic, aesthetic and other considerations dictate the basic characteristics of each dance. To paraphrase Kwabena Nketia, what may be considered proper and beautiful and, therefore acceptable in a dance from one area or in a particular period, may be deemed unacceptable in another (Nketia1966: 22). It depends on the circumstances and factors that gave birth to the particular dance form. The creators of dance usually introduce their new dances to the community for public approval.

In Ghana, many communities hold their traditional rulers in high esteem. Citizens regard these leaders as custodians of culture and the arts. Tradition requires that the king, chief or a queen-mother be able to dance and understand the gestures and meaning of the dance. Their subjects also expect them to be conversant with music of the dance and to be able to interpret the language of the drums, poetry and proverbs of their people. So, before ascending to that high office, the candidate learns the intricacies of his or her community's dance traditions.

To appreciate and evaluate the dance, one must look at its functions, its symbolic meaning and aesthetic qualities. Also, in many Ghanaian communities it is only when such dance creations conform to the norms of the community's dance traditions that the dance earns the community's approval. Additionally, groups from neighbouring towns and villages usually 'borrow' dance movements or whole dance forms from one other. Such borrowers add new movements to the dance. They use their own dance experiences to expand the rhythmic interpretations and other relevant elements, creating new dance forms of their own. It is worth noting that the various communities do not usually analyse or formally discuss aesthetics and other norms of traditional societies in Ghana, nor indeed in many parts of Africa. Rather, manifestations of these norms in legends, folk tales, songs and riddles, and of course dance occur through one's experience of participating in such events and the support the individual receives from community members.

Traditional ruler dancing in a palanquin

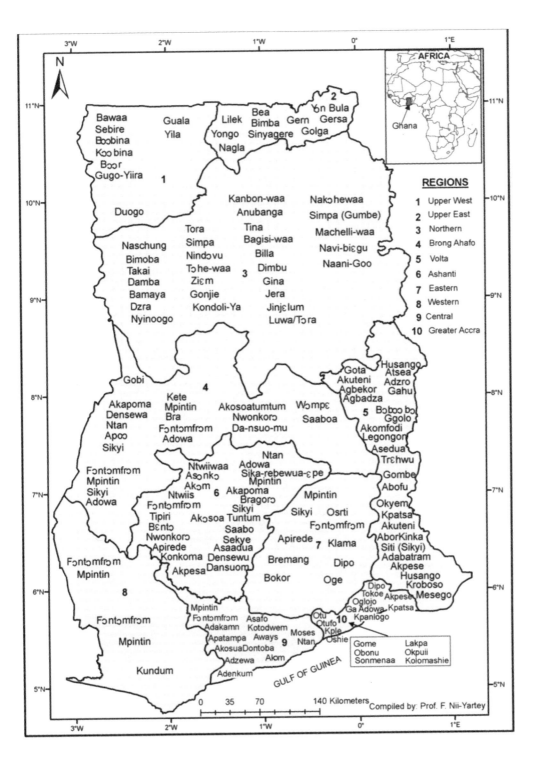

An incomplete regional dance map of Ghana

African Dance in Ghana: Contemporary Transformations

CHAPTER 3

Choreographic and Aesthetic Principles

The responsibility of dance creation, though, falls on a few creative and active individuals and certain social groups and households that may have been assigned this responsibility. According to Nketia,

> "...Some art forms (are) associated with the community as a whole, certain expressions (are) linked with social groups within it – social groups distinguished on the basis of sex or age, or on the basis (of) kinship affiliations, or on the basis of association – as warriors, devotees of cults or members of occupational groups such as fishermen or elephant hunters. There are also forms that (are) linked to the royal court. ... The process of socialisation or enculturation (enables) the individual to acquire his (or her) knowledge of (dance) and skills needed to fulfil his (or her) role as a member of his (or her) society or to fulfil his (or her) obligation as a custodian or carrier of a particular tradition..." (Nketia 1970. Pp. 71)

However, the outcome and ownership of such creative pursuits is not usually attributed to the individual creator but rather considered a community property. Different categories of dance genres represent the various communities. Some dances are performed occasionally and reserved for specific individuals and special groups associated with royalty. In many cases, even within the royal domain, not everybody may perform certain royal dances. Thus, the *Kete* royal dance of the Ashanti of Ghana was originally the preserve of the king and his wives, while only specific sections of the *Obonu* royal dance of the Ga may be performed by a dancer on the lower scale of the royal ladder.

In religious dances, however, one must be 'chosen' by a particular deity to qualify to dance. The dance, in this case, is a gift from the gods to the community through the priest or priestess. So usually the priests or the priestesses serve as mediums, and occasionally their assistants and advisors perform. But everybody has a role in the performance, so the rest of the community may help with providing music or aspects of rituals associated with the performance. In occupational dances for men, such as the *Abofoo* of the Ivory Coast and Ghana or the *Inakpale* of Togo, one may have to belong to a guild of hunters (either as a professional hunter or a position one has inherited from family tradition) to participate in these dances.

Male war veterans usually perform in dances associated with war. In some cases individual women with outstanding courage and ability may perform dances connected with war. Yaa Asantewa of Ghana and Queen Amina of Nigeria are historical examples of such women. Women usually perform special ritual dances at home when the men have gone to war to ensure victory for the latter. Patience Kwakwa (1994) observes that,

> " ... In Asante there is a most interesting female dance ritual which, in the past, took place during periods of crisis such as outbreak of war and epidemics. The mothers, sisters, wives and daughters of the fighting men ... took charge of affairs at home ... to fight a spiritual warfare on behalf of the men. This ... took the form of a processional dance ritual, *mmobome. Mmobome* combines song, hand clapping, dance, and ritual performances..." (p.12)

In Zimbabwe, both men and women perform the *Muchongoyo* dance in preparation for war and celebration of victory. The men perform the main and more energetic movements, while the women do improvised shuffling movements and help with the playing of musical instruments and singing (Kariamu Welsh: 1994, p. 216). Participation in some traditional warrior dances, like the *Asafo* of the Fante of Ghana, is based on automatic patrilineal inheritance for both men and women.

Often, such factors as social, religious and historical situations; ecological, environmental and climatic conditions; and other considerations dictate the basic characteristics of a dance. Mawere-Opoku (1966) defines choreography from an African perspective as,

> "...The putting together of carefully selected movements which express clear ideas, a style or character combined with form ... drum rhythms, voices, costumes, and mimed gestures etc..." (p.53)

In addition to the above definition, which is similar to the universal definition of choreography, the function, aesthetic quality, symbolic and contextual significance of each dance genre in the African context are of paramount importance and interest to the community. Components of the dances are the result of formalised and consciously manipulated cultural and social patterns like holding, pounding, greetings, hoeing and others are referred to as "the movement aspects of customary behaviour". They become resources which the dance creator uses.

To create a dance piece depends on the circumstances and factors that gave birth to the particular dance genre. Invariably, it is only when such dance creations conform to the canons of the community's dance traditions that the dance so created earns approval. Even though each dance evolves its own technique and rules, the basic norms (among others) listed below guide the appreciation and evaluation of dance in many African communities.

According to Nketia, (1970) traditional African dances usually are created by homogenous communities:

" ... In the artistic languages and idioms of the community by artists who belong to it and are enjoyed by those who have learned the languages in which they are communicated." (p. 71)

Farris Thompson (1983: xiii) also observed that

" ...much of the popular music of the world is informed by the flash of the spirit of a certain people [Africans] specially armed with improvisatory drive and brilliance..."

He went on:

"Ancient African organising principles of song and dance have crossed the seas from the old world to the new world..... They took on new momentum, intermingling with each other."

These principles include: "The dominance of a percussive style (attack and vital aliveness in sound and motion); a propensity for multiple meter (competing meters sounding all at once); overlapping call and response in singing (solo/chorus – voice/instrument – interlock system of performance); inner pulse control (a metronome sense, keeping a beat indelibly in mind as rhythmic common denominator in a welter of different meters); suspended accentuation patterning (off-beat phrasing of melodic and choreographic accents)..."

Here are a few examples of the requirements and principles guiding the performing arts, useful in understanding our artistic forms:

1. constant improvisation within the structure of the dance
2. creativity within the dance
3. freedom of individual expression
4. emotional input by participants
5. basic maintenance of rounded body and relaxed knees
6. limited exaggeration of movement
7. repetition of basic movements
8. contextual reference to the dance
9. simultaneous use of several movements and rhythms
10. the use of appropriate gestures in the dance
11. inter-relationship between music and dance.

Improvisation and Repetition

African world view reflects a continuity of experience and a recurring relationship between the past and the present; the ancestors and the living; the unexpected and the familiar. Repetition and improvisation are products of this concept, together recapturing the dance's dramatic moments to help refresh and heighten the communal experience. Alphonse Tierou (1989a) observes that:

> "...Africans tend to be uninterested in any art that lacks improvisation. ... Every innovation and creation involves a thorough knowledge of technique which can then be 'forgotten' in order to allow spontaneous personal interpretations ... In every traditional African dance the dancer is free to improvise because traditional African dances depend both on the repetition of the basic movements on *and* improvisation around those movements ... Improvisation in Africa is not a result, as in the West, of spontaneity but much more of the creative imagination of the improviser who applies himself to a given subject known to everybody..." (p. 18-19)

The spontaneity and personal interpretation with which the dancer performs, and his or her ability to recapitulate the shared values of the dance, contribute to the overall aesthetic of the performance.

Circular Images and Symbolism

The notion of beauty in body posture is conceptualised in terms of 'curves' and other circular images. The body is almost always slightly rounded, the knees relaxed, while the movement is earth-bound. The belief is that circular images give a sense of perpetual motion and completeness of being. To appreciate the dance therefore, one also must understand the symbolism of the occasion. This includes the meaning of the gestures, the significance of costumes and their colours, the meaning of the accompanying song lyrics, the implications of the drum language and, of course, the dramatic requirements of the event.

Limited Exaggeration of Movement

Many African dance movements tend to follow the natural functions and form of the body. Any unexplained departure from this basic concept, by over-stretching or extension or any form of rigidity is viewed as exaggeration, and therefore considered aesthetically inappropriate. This approach may differ slightly among communities. Sometimes, emphasising a quality of movement such as strong or subtle, rippling or jerking a specific part or parts of the body may be preferred over others in a particular community to indicate the basic characteristics of dances in that community. Kwakwa (1994) and others have observed, for example, that

> "...the Akan people of Ghana emphasise the use of the arms, hands and feet in their dances... the Anglo Ewe of Ghana and those of neighbouring countries, the Republics of Togo and Benin, concentrate on movements of the upper torso in their dances..." (p. 11)

A typical rounded-body position in Ghanaian dance

Similarly, in the dances of the *Lobi* of Northern Ghana, the upper torso is brought into prominence in the *Sebre* dance while the Frafra also from the same region, prefer a combination of arms, shoulder movements and foot stamping in the *Bima* dance.

Contextual Reference to Dance

A particular dance may be performed under different contexts. A dance performance may take place in the open – the court yard of the king, the grounds of the shrine, the compound of a household, etc. It may be performed at a wedding ceremony or at a funeral. In each case, the dynamics of the dance movements, facial expressions, gestures, the rhythm, the accompanying songs and other details – reflect the specific context in which the dance takes place.

Thus, the royal *Obonu* dance of the Ga people may be performed during the funeral of a royal or a prominent member of the community, using movements denoting the sad nature of the occasion and the good or bad deeds and other attributes of the deceased. On another occasion, such as the celebration of war victory, the same dance might be performed with a different set of movements and gestures. In this case more aggressive movements are employed, expressing battle motifs and creating the general atmosphere of a battle scene. In each case, the text, mood and rhythmic patterns played on the drums may differ.

Multiple Movements

In the Ghanaian dance tradition, weight and centre are established through the pelvis and manifested in the hips, while the various parts of the body together perform simultaneously with different movements, speeds and qualities in multiple directions to create a harmonious and organic whole. This combination fosters power and economy of movement to help evoke the dance's important aesthetic qualities and meaning. The knees are flexed, the feet well-grounded and the arms rounded. From these basic positions, the dancers extend, contract and contrast to define the core movements emanating from the torso and the pelvic regions – the centre.

This dynamic interplay of energy, time, gravity and rhythm usually manifests itself in the movement qualities society assigns to men and women, the old and the young, the king and the ordinary citizen. This dictates how the dancer in each dance genre and context should employ these. In the *Adowa* dance of the Ashanti, for example, a female solo dancer uses various parts of her body, including her head, to correspond to rhythmic patterns while her feet and hands may be moving independently in different directions. In this case, movement of the torso articulates the subtle movements of the pelvic region while it performs its own independent movements. When the *Adowa* dance is performed in pairs, the dancers may relate their movements to each other in a reciprocal manner, or they may decide to interact with the spectators instead. Also of great importance in African dance creation and performance is that the choreographer be a good dancer, because

" ...the ability to express oneself competently and to communicate ideas, emotions, and knowledge through the language of dance is recognised as an important attribute of a cultured, educated citizen... training lasts throughout the dancer's lifetime. A sense of rhythm and timing are taught through voice simulations of drumming with hand clapping, miming to work chants, and the recitation of dramatic incidents in folk tales at storytelling sessions. This sustained training programme makes it possible for a dancer to meet several dance situations, even the most technically demanding..." (Mawere-Opoku 1987, p. 194)

In addition to the above, choreographic knowledge and craft are acquired through kinetic experience gained from common activities and behaviours. For example, complex rhythmic combinations in African recreational activities such as the Ghanaian *Nteewa* hand clapping and *Ampe* multi-rhythmic games for women, and *Djama*, a rhythmic game-of-strength for men, help to instil a rhythmic sense, movement awareness, discipline and trust in the dancer from an early age. Later in life, re-enactments of past events such as hunting expeditions, wars, ceremonial rituals and festivals and story-telling sessions provide resources for creative and technical foundation for dance creation.

Relationship of Music and Dance

In Africa it is often said that, "when the beats of the drums die down, usually the dancing also ceases" (Nketia 1963, p.163) and in many cases, names of musical and dance types are used interchangeably. For example, the *Kolomashie* of the Ga people and the *Eseni Ogbo* of the Ijaw of Nigeria are considered both musical and dance types. "Rhythm remains the central core to any expression of African culture and consequently the centre of any analysis that is conducted..." (Kariamu Welsh: 1998 p. 207) Usually the rhythm determines the structure and sequence of the dance. Depending on the requirements of the dance and the complexity of the music that accompanies its performance, the rhythmic patterns may be melodic or percussive linearly or multi-linearly.

The dancer therefore looks for the primary regulative beats of the music for his (or her) performance. He (or she) then builds on these and other musical elements like speed, time and alternative rhythmic patterns provided by supporting instruments to phrase and elaborate his (or her) movements to help develop his (or her) performance.

Use of Dramatic Elements

Even though most traditional African dances are abstract in a larger sense, there is always some kind of story – either personal or based on community experience. Nketia (1988 b) has observed three kinds of dramatic forms in traditional African society:

> "...'ceremonial' drama – dramatic expression associated with social, ritual or ceremonial occasions. 'Narrative' drama, a composite of speech (narrative and dialogue) music and mime... It finds its most elaborate expression in... story-telling... 'dance-drama'...expressed through music, poetry, mime and movements of dance..." (p. 29)

Dance in its various forms is an inextricable part of all three categories. In the *Adevu* hunters' dance of the Ewe of Ghana, for example, a sudden and abrupt stop or an intuitive emotional outburst during the performance may underline the motivation, mood and characterisation behind a personal experience on a hunting expedition. *Adevu* which is a traditional dance–drama is full of unexpected dramatic moments and tension accompanied by appropriate facial expressions, movements, drumming and songs to narrate the hunter's experiences.

The dancer's actions are characterised by slow, fast and sudden stops as he stalks his prey. He takes short, rhythmic but careful steps in a crouching position, his face focused in the direction of the elusive animal. Suddenly his movement pattern changes when the difficulty of locating the animal is resolved.

Through his performance, the dancer invites the spectators into his world of anxiety in locating his prey and his disappointment when he fails to kill the imaginary animal on the first attempt. When he finally succeeds, his movements become bigger and outward and more expressive.

Costumes and their Relevance

One important aspect of the African tradition is the variety of costumes – their colours and the role colours play in identifying social roles of community members and enhancing the various social activities, including different dance forms. Other factors like the social, political and the financial status of the people influence the costumes they wear. In Ghana, men in the northern sector of the country traditionally wear smocks over pantaloons, while men in the southern part of the country prefer eight to nine yards of cloth, worn half behind the body, and half in front of the body.

The right half is then thrown over the left shoulder, leaving the other shoulder exposed.

Typical male and female costumes in northern Ghana

A pair of ahenemma (sandals) and a pair of shorts are worn, to complete the outfit. With few exceptions, however, women in Ghana traditionally dress the same. Two separate pieces of cloth, (ntoma) measuring two yards each are used; as an under-cloth over which the other is wrapped. A blouse-like top (kaba) is added to match.

However, it is in the dance that costumes are animated and brought to life. According to Nketia:

"There are roles for individuals – priests, chiefs, elders, heads of families, officials of the court such as spokesmen, executioners, court criers, drummers, (dancers and queen mothers) etc. Each person comes properly dressed or wearing the costume that marks his (or her) office or special role in the drama of the occasion. … Costumes may similarly be conceived as part of the movement complex – as extensions of body curves or circles and spins described by the dancer or as extensions of arm movements… suggests or dictates the flow of movement in order to create shapes in space … as for example in some of the dances (*Takai* and *Bamaaya*) of the Dagbani in which long flowing robes or smocks (and Yelpsa waist gear) are worn…Dance costume may also be selected for the purpose of creating an atmosphere or for conveying a message through the symbolism of their colours, shapes or details of design…" (1988, p. 23- 31)

Performers may be elaborately or scantily dressed, depending on the requirements of the particular dance. Some dances are designed to reveal certain parts of the body in order to draw attention to the details of particular movements, as in the *Sebre* dance of the Lobi of Ghana, where the main focus of the dance is on the vibrating movements of the upper torso. Elaborate costumes can disguise the dancer's identity as he takes on the role of a spiritual entity in the *Bolohi* panthers' dance, performed at the enthronement and funeral ceremonies of the Snuff of the Ivory Coast.

If the occasion is sad or serious, such as a funeral, or occurs in times of conflict, dark colours such as black, red, russet-brown and other earthy colours are preferred. If it is a happy social event, the predominant colours will be white, light or bright colours. Additionally, the style of

Traditional priests on their way to the shrine

costumes for particular events is carefully chosen to reflect the spirit and decorum of the occasion. According to Kwame Gyeke (1996):

> "The quality, style, or cut of a dress must always be appropriate to the occasion. A woman who is appropriately dressed for a great occasion is highly appreciated; but a woman must not overdress for a simple occasion or she will be ridiculed." (p.128)

Wearing clothing and other adornments in a manner other than what society has prescribed is considered disrespectful and rebellious against particular individuals or society as a whole.

Props and their Relevance

The use of such implements as bows and arrows, horse or cow tails, wooden staffs and similar items in some traditional dances for historical and identification purposes – or for aesthetic reasons – is evident in many parts of Africa. For example, in the *Lilek* dance the performers use bows and arrows to re-enact how the Builsa people of northern Ghana defended themselves against slave raiders during the 18th century.

Apart from their aesthetic value, the use of such implements may also confirm a belief held by some communities that the horsetail or cow's tail contains spiritual powers and therefore helps protect the user against spiritual reprisals by enemies. Their use also identifies social positions and ancestral connections of community members. For example, in the *Nakwaawa* butchers' dance of the Dagomba of Northern Ghana, a horse's tail plays a significant part.

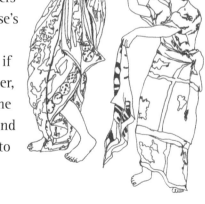

The Dagomba are patrilineal; therefore, if one's father or one's mother's father is a butcher, one is qualified to perform the *Nakwaawa*. The dancer holds the horsetail with the left hand and raises it above the head while performing to indicate that he or she inherited the position

Typical male and female custumes in southern Ghana

through the mother's family. If the inheritance is directly through the father's lineage, the dancer performs holding the horsetail with the right hand raised above the head. The use of such special items in dance and other social situations is limitless in African communities.

Make-Up and its Relevance

Make-up in Ghanaian dances by choice is deliberately not as elaborate as one finds in other parts of Africa, except in the religious and initiation dances. The *Akom* and *Kple* religious dances and *Dipo* and *Otufo* puberty dances of the Ga-Damgbe people are typical examples, where sometimes the whole face, torso, arms and legs of the dancers are smeared with ayeloo (white clay). Markings of ntsuma (red clay) on specific parts of the body are associated with funerals and war situations, while ayelo and kloboo smearing is identified with festive and ceremonial occasions. Among the Dagomba and other ethnic groups of northern Ghana, kooli, a shiny grey powdery substance, believed to help maintain healthy eyelashes, is used to decorate the eyelids while lenle (made from the henna leaf) is used to dye the feet of married women.

Traditional African knowledge, wisdom and values discussed above are encoded in various ceremonies, festivals, story-telling sessions, proverbs and other social occurrences – and in all these, dance plays a significant role. Frequent active participation in these activities by community members often helps nourish and extend the life span of the various artistic forms and ultimately ensures their preservation.

Traditional body markings among the Ga people

Symbolic Hat Positions in Northern Ghana

1 When the top of the hat is upright: *"I am in charge here!"*
2 When the hat falls on the left side of the wearer: *"I can see all enemies on my left."*
3 When the hat falls on the right side of the wearer: *"I can see all enemies on my right."*
4 When the hat falls in front of the wearer: *"I can see all enemies ahead of me."*
5 When the hat falls back of the wearer: *"I can see all enemies behind me."*

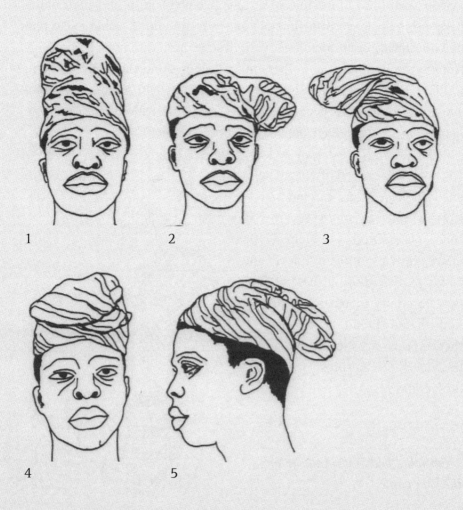

1   2   3

4   5

CHAPTER 4

The New Paradigm

The advent of colonisation and, in more recent times globalisation, have in their wake increased the mobility of people and services, technological advancement, capital and labour across ethnic, regional and national boundaries with tremendously varied effects on the artistic and cultural practices of the people. Consequently, the language of dance is expanding as new movements' vocabulary and themes emerge to articulate the current experiences and trends of the communities. Similarly, the exposure of local arts and artists to foreign artistic forms and values, and to formal education based principally on Western models, has helped create a climate of interesting innovations in the Ghanaian artistic milieu.

Organised concert dance performance in Ghana, for example, began nearly five years into the country's independence. The factors, ideas and events that led to the establishment of many artistic and cultural institutions in Ghana, according to Efua Sutherland, were defined by the National Theatre Movement, conceived in the 1950s to help bridge the gap between theoretical knowledge and practice in the performing arts. The National Theatre Movement also created viable forms of music, dance and drama. (Efua Sutherland 2000:45)

Many considered Ghana's first president, Dr Kwame Nkrumah, as a man of culture and a committed Pan Africanist, who was determined to help reverse the legacy of Ghana's slavery and colonial past. Nkrumah recognised the potential of the arts and culture in the new nation's development. In 1962 he approved the establishment of the Ghana Institute of Arts and Culture.

The Institute operated directly under the office of the president to advice government on cultural and artistic issues. In 1968, the Arts Council of Ghana officially took over the work of the institute.

The Arts Council was mandated to promote and encourage appreciation of the arts; in particular, to preserve, foster and develop the traditional arts and culture of Ghana.

The Arts Council's activities included the establishment and maintenance of a National Theatre, a National Orchestra and Choir (now known as the National Symphony Orchestra), a National Art and Craft Gallery and a Dance Ensemble. It also maintained a Folkloric Company and an affiliated relationship with a number of amateur dance groups, many of them resident in Accra (Apronti/Akyea 1969:104). The establishment of the Folkloric Company was a later development. The Arts Council decided to create its own resident dance group when its leadership could not see eye-to-eye with the leadership of the Institute of African Studies based at the University of Ghana, Legon, over the artistic direction the Ghana Dance Ensemble (under the Institute of African Studies) should take. For many years, the relationship between the institutions was everything but cordial. The Ghana Dance Ensemble's

Institute of Arts and Culture, Accra

success, based on its research and programme activities, led eventually to the integration of the Folkloric Company into the Ghana Dance Ensemble in 1986.

Many workplace artistic groups were established in the country during the 1960s, including the Osagyefo Players, a theatre group made up of some of the country's best actors. The Workers' Brigade, and the Young Pioneer Movement and others, maintained their own performing groups. Nkrumah showed personal interest in the construction of the Ghana Drama Studio by Efua Sutherland, which incidentally occupied the spot in Accra on which the National Theatre stands today. According to J H Kwabena Nketia, one of Nkrumah's key advisors and programme implementers, the President gave these institutions and programmes generous moral and financial support to help them restore and develop the arts and culture of Ghana and Africa. In 1989, the mandate of the Arts Council was taken over by a newly established National Commission on Culture; its offices became the Greater Accra Regional Centre for National Culture.

The Institute of African Studies was established in 1961 and mandated to check the accuracy of written accounts of Africa's past, and to help preserve the intrinsic values of the arts and culture of the continent. This involved re-interpreting and re-assessing components of the African past; and helping ensure the kind of education which produces devoted men and women with imagination, ideas, and inspiration. It paid particular attention to the arts of Africa for the enhancement and understanding of African institutions, values and cultural bonds. (Kwame Nkrumah1963)

"In 1962 the establishment of the Ghana Dance Ensemble began in a very modest way as a collaboration between a government department: the Ghana Institute of Arts and Culture primarily concerned with promotion of the arts and a University of Ghana department – the Institute of African Studies – the nation's first academic institution dedicated to African research and teaching. The Ghana Dance Ensemble continued to provide leadership for practical neo-traditional dance training at the University of Ghana, in addition to its functions as a repository of Ghanaian and African dances and a laboratory for fellows of the Institute. A major achievement of the Dance Ensemble is the ability of its leaders over the years to ensure that the study and teaching of the traditional remained faithful to the traditions of the communities while at the same time meeting the challenges posed by the modern theatre." (Nketia 1967)

In establishing the Dance Ensemble, a School of Music, Dance and Drama (now the School of Performing Arts) was also set up to train professional dancers, musicians and actors, to offer opportunities for dance education and to ensure continuity in the dance traditions of Ghana and Africa. Ofotsu Adinku observed that the training programme of the School of Music and Drama, "which initially was supposed to be African-centred", included courses in modern dance technique, labanotation and modern theatre technique, such as stage lighting, in addition to indigenous subjects like African dance forms.

Both Ghanaian and foreign teachers taught these courses, a visionary practice which encouraged the training of cultural administrators and the rapid promotion and development of many cultural institutions and programmes. The Institute of African Studies also set the pace for other African countries and further developed other forms of dance expression in Ghana. Several students from other African countries benefited from the experiences offered by the institute, and many amateur dance groups sprang up, especially in the regional capitals. These groups modelled their dance presentations on the neo-traditional dance repertoire of the Ghana Dance Ensemble.

Neo-Traditional Dance

This cultural re-awakening led to a second phase: the neo-traditional dance genre in Ghana was under the direction of Mawere-Opoku and J H Kwabena Nketia. Although the events culminating in this rapid development of dance in Ghana sometimes appeared scattered and unconnected, they resulted from Nkrumah's cultural initiative to re-light the torch of the African consciousness in what he termed "the African Personality and African Genius" in the 1960s.

The Author with Professor A Mawere-Opoku (left) and Professor J H K Nketia (right)

Mawere-Opoku brought together existing traditional dances from around the country and carefully re-arranged their movements outside their usual rural community contexts to suit the conventional stage. He explored related art forms such as music and painting, as well as costumes, props and the principles of traditional dance performance from individual ethnic groups. He organised them to suit the taste of his mixed audiences by shortening the repetitions that characterise some of the dances in their original forms. The dancers, who usually dance towards the musicians or are encircled by the latter during the performance, were re-directed to dance facing different directions. This allowed more visibility of the body's movements from different angles. Important movements, which otherwise may not have attracted the attention of the usually mixed audiences, were also 'amplified' for clarity and so on.

Dance-theatre and Contemporary Dance

Following this development, two new forms have emerged and exist side-by-side with the traditional and neo-traditional forms: dance-theatre and contemporary dance. The traditional form represents the first of these stages. It draws its existence from communal experiences and needs. These experiences dictate the form and content of dance creation and practice. Traditional dance development and training is relatively slower and less formal in approach than the neo-traditional and contemporary forms. Collective inputs are paramount in traditional dance creation and very rarely are creations of any particular dance form attributed to individuals.

The emergence of a distinct Ghanaian dance-theatre arose from the employment of modern production methods. It did much to integrate the many factors represented in the dance into a coherent unity of expression of the theme as felt by the choreographer, the dancers and the audience. The first serious dance-theatre production in Ghana was Mawere-Opoku's African *Liberation Dance Suite* (1965). It is set in five movements – exploitation and enslavement of Africa; the awakening and call to arms; lamentation for the dead freedom fighters; struggle for freedom, and celebration of victory. This work achieved a concise but full and clear dance presentation. It merged Western and traditional Ghanaian theatre concepts in a way that allowed for flexibility, variety and fluidity.

Lamentation for Freedom Fighters

The following notes by Mawere-Opoku illustrate the power of the choreography. The most powerful movement in the choreography is the *Lamentation for Freedom Fighters*. A grave, deeply moving and dignified dance, it serves as the focus for Opoku's masterpiece.

> "The piece opens with a darkened stage with drummers and drums in silhouette.
> Bells – sound softly – a song to Yeve gong played on the thighs to create echoes.
> A series of polyrhythmic musical sounds join in the build-up. ...A procession of
> singers – walk on stage with arm gestures, folding across and opening. A group of

priests and priestesses position themselves in the center of the procession. They form a chorus around the drummers. The priests move in front of the chorus while the priestesses form a semi-circle. At the sound of the drums, they fall on their knees except priests.

"Responding to a sign from the chief priest, all the priestesses run off stage, screaming and wringing their hands. The bells of the *Husago* music slowly, gravely, gradually diminish into a faint resonance but clearer and nearer as the priestesses return. The priestesses go into a lamentation; the chorus responds with rocking body movements from side to side, contracting, and releasing the torso in prostrate posture. Finally, the figure leads into *Husago* male and female partnership, ultimately taking on a symbolic expression of sorrow and deep emotion. The Akyea segment of the piece is sometimes sad and tender, then wild, strong and gay. The finale of the suite is dramatised through the *Agbekor* warrior dance of the Ewe of south-eastern Ghana." (Mawere-Opoku 80)

These laudable achievements in dance presentation did not, however, meet the expectations of some critics within and outside the University of Ghana. They voiced concerns about what they saw as Westernisation of traditional Ghanaian dance forms. These concerns came at a time when, according to Ofotsu Adinku, "there were problems because some members of the University of Ghana, which was hosting the Institute of African Studies, were themselves not accustomed to a cultural programme that brought local priests, musicians, and dancers from the ethnic system to the campus to interact with students". (Adinku 2004:49) The critics contended that the traditional dance forms should remain pure, regardless of the impact of many years' interaction with the outside world. These complaints and attitudes, however, were short-lived as the work of the Institute surpassed the expectations of many traditional Ghanaians.

The overwhelming success of the *African Liberation Dance Suite* opened the floodgates for the creation of dance-theatre works like *The Lost Warrior*, the *King's Dilemma*, *Bukom* and *The Legend of Okoryoo*, all by Nii-Yartey.

The Legend of Okoryoo was another landmark in Ghana's history of dance-theatre development. Okoryoo, the principal character in this piece, represents the perfect woman and a messenger of peace. She emerges from a giant egg. Her first divine mission after she is hatched is to help other eggs to hatch within a specific time. Other celestial messengers will emerge, and together they will bring peace, love and development to the human race. Failing to hatch the eggs after prolonged attempts, Okoryoo sets out alone to Earth to accomplish what should have been a collective task.

The stage opens with a weird mixture of atmospheric, cosmic elements – darkness, blustering winds, roaring waves, thunder, lightning and the haunting cries of forlorn birds, composed by William Anku. This sets the stage for an eerie tale of prophesies, creation, intrigue, betrayal, annihilation and ultimate reincarnation, the theme for this dance-theatre. The effect is both magical and ritualistic. Sometimes, the performance becomes sombre, fraught with compassion for the resilient Okoryoo, who is condemned to death for her inability to continue giving to mankind – an unfitting reward for her generosity. Apart from the aesthetic nature of the costumes and lighting, human moods are presented by sound effects.

The tempo of sound, produced largely by drummers, determines whether a particular situation depicts a reflective mood or a specific action. Sporadic flashes of light on the cyclorama synchronise perfectly with the action to portray the different moods and emotions in choreography.

The Maidens by Patience Kwakwa, *The Orphan* by Ofotsu Adinku, *Nsrabo* by Doudu Ampofo, *Odwira* by Asare Newman and *Ajamutukalee* by Oh! Nii Kwei Sowah. All these choreographic pieces in many respects, followed in the footsteps of Mawere-Opoku's *African Liberation Dance Suite.*

Today, works of the Nii-Yarteys, Adinkus, Kwakwas and others are influencing a new generation of choreographers, ensuring a future of vibrant creativity and development of dance in Ghana. Notable among these young people are Benjamin Ayeetey, Joshua Trebi, Okuley Tetteh,

Terry Bright Ofosu, Nii-Tete Yartey, David Quaye, Naa Ayeley Okine, Yawuza Alhassan and others.

In the 1980s a young man named Frank Idun helped revive the Miss Ghana pageant, after a twenty-year absence, along with a novelty: a dance championship. The two events took place on the same night and it was dubbed the 'Double Do' sponsored by Pioneer Tobacco Company. The author of this book directed and served as chief judge for the dance segment of the Double Do. Initially, the dance competition centred mainly on dance movements popularised on television and video by Michael Jackson, M C Hammer and other Americans.

Some traditionalists who witnessed the first event seriously objected to what obviously seemed to represent Western culture and values. This criticism strengthened the dance director's position that, as part of the qualifying process, each contestant must perform, at the national finals at least, one traditional Ghanaian dance. The argument against this position was that traditional dance was not required at the Malibu World Dance Championship in London where the national champion would compete. The condition that the contestants perform a traditional dance was accepted only by some of the organisers insofar as this would get the critics off everybody's backs. It was not too difficult the following year to get everybody to concur with another dimension of the dance event. Every contestant was required to perform the free-style, one traditional dance and top it off with a combination of the two dance forms. It was electrifying. As a result of the achievements and the conducive atmosphere created by the Double Do Dance competition and other events during the period, a young man, Adjetey Sowah, won the world championship in London with a dazzling combination of the traditional *Highlife*, *Kpanlogo* and free style dance movements, laced with simulations of motorbike riding and movements associated with other everyday activities of contemporary life.

The number of competitors increased over time, and the public's interest grew as the quality of dancing improved. The value of the winners' prize shot up from a million or so Cedis, a few packages of '555' cigarettes and a couple of T-shirts, to a motorbike and, eventually, a car. Many youths looked forward to the dance championship and spent almost the whole year training and perfecting their dance routines. Many of them became professionals. Unfortunately, the flow of sponsorship packages decreased when the main sponsors, Pioneer Tobacco Company, pulled out when tobacco sales waned. Even though other franchise holders and sponsors tried under different names and managements to continue with the event, things did not work out well. Eventually the dance component of the Miss Ghana pageant was phased out. However, the ideas, the creative energies and interest generated by the event and most important of all, the number of young dancers it produced helped shape the way modern dance is perceived in Ghana today.

A free-style dance competition between Terry Bright Ofosu and Derrick Essuman at the Star Hotel in Accra, 1989

The National Theatre

The National Theatre building in Accra was envisaged to showcase the achievements of the National Theatre Movement. For the right or the wrong reasons, however, before construction of the National Theatre was commissioned in 1992, the government decided that since funding for the National Symphony Orchestra, the Ghana Dance Ensemble and the Abibigromma Theatre Company also came from government coffers; it had the right to house these national performing arts companies at the National Theatre.

The Ghana National Theatre Law 1991 (PNDCL 259), legitimised this arrangement. The official opening of the National Theatre was as highly successful as it was eventful. All the above named national performing institutions, performed in a production based on Kwame Nkrumah's concept of the 'African Genius', scripted by W Tamakloe and Ben Abdallah, and choreographed by F Nii-Yartey. *The African Genius* is a story that seeks to chronicle the policy set in motion in Ghana to project and maintain the personality of the African with a message that, "without a cultural base, no country can grow socially, economically and politically".

Unfortunately, what could have been, historically and artistically, a significant arrangement for arts and artistes of the institutions involved, and indeed Ghanaian artists generally, turned sour. The government did not adequately and 'properly' communicate with the University of Ghana's authorities where the country's formal artistic training was nurtured. Many felt the government worked to intimidate the university authorities to hand over control of performing groups they had established and nurtured and which were integral to the university's teaching and research activities. Many applauded the university's firm refusal to allow part of it to be taken away by what was considered political high-handedness rather than a progressive arrangement.

Some people supported the notion that the groups were a legitimate part of the university system and that the government should set up its own dance and theatre companies for the newly established National Theatre. To some others, the university authorities were just being difficult and uncooperative. After all, the work of any university is to train people for national development, they argued. Whatever positions were held in the matter, the fact remains that proper development of the arts and arts personnel should always be above personal and institutional interests. It should symbolise and mark the fulfilment of the aspirations of Ghanaians.

The director of the Ghana Dance Ensemble took a leave of absence from the University of Ghana. Guest artists and a few older members of the Ghana Dance Ensemble followed him to the National Theatre. This undertaking, despite all the misunderstandings, was not only remarkable and far-reaching in the history of dance development in Ghana, but significant also for changes in the way dance was created and presented following in the footsteps of Mawere-Opoku.

Within three years, the new offshoot of the Ghana Dance Ensemble had trained the relatively young dancers brought to the theatre and was ready to significantly change the way Ghanaians perceived dance as theatre. For purposes of differentiation, the Dance Ensemble at the National Theatre used The National Dance Company of Ghana as a sub-name. At the time, it was thought necessary to use the name this way instead of changing it completely because of obvious legal and other implications, not only in accessing crucial government funding, but also because negotiations were still going on between government and the university at the time.

After a period it became clear that the country would have two national dance companies: The Ghana Dance Ensemble and The National Dance Company of Ghana. Although the legal issues were still outstanding, the group at the National Theatre continued to use the name 'The National Dance Company of Ghana' – an unofficial arrangement acceptable to some. Most of the neo-traditional dance repertoire developed at the University of Ghana by Mawere-Opoku was maintained by the group at the National Theatre. However within two years of its inception, the National Dance Company had carved for itself a vibrant artistic reputation in the country and beyond, with productions of high quality and innovative stage setting and properties. The company had the advantage of the right facilities and a more 'professional' environment for its work. Furthermore, there were fewer administrative bottlenecks and less interference in professional discipline of the company. These advantages are among the most important requirements for meaningful development of any professional company.

The rapid development characterising the work of the National Dance Company of Ghana at the theatre reflected how government and the university could have benefited, had each realised that they needed each other to fulfil their specific mandates. Unfortunately, both sides did not fully realise this. Furthermore, the development of dance and all stakeholders was compromised in the process.

At the National Theatre, major international collaborative dance productions became part of the National Dance Company's programmes, involving primarily choreographers from Africa and the African Diaspora. Ironically, the first choreographer was French. The French cultural attaché in Ghana had been impressed with the company's dance-theatre production, *The Legend of Okoryoo*, and had decided to support its efforts. To qualify for available funds it was required to have French artistic involvement at some level. The compromise was either to bring a music composer or scenic designer to collaborate with a Ghanaian choreographer. The company opted for a French choreographer.

Serious national and international touring by The National Dance Company of Ghana, resumed in 1996 after many years of inactivity. Foreign institutions began to sponsor and commission dance productions in the country. Major dance productions, formerly only seen in major theatres outside the country, became part of the Ghanaian dance scene. *Solma*, by Nii-Yartey and Jean-François Duroure; *Musu – Saga of the Slaves*, by Nii-Yartey and Monty Thompson; *Images of Conflict*, by Nii-Yartey and Germaine Acogny; *Children of Fate*, by Nanna Nielson and Nii-Yartey; and *The Power Within* by 'H' Patten and Nii-Yartey, to name a few, lifted dance to a new level.

Choreographing sporting event ceremonies

At another level, dance and sports combined for the first time in a significant way to create a spectacle of movement, football, colour and excitement. The choreographic work for the opening and closing ceremonies of the Africa Under-20 Football finals held in Accra, dubbed GHANA 99; and the finals of the Africa Cup of Nations, CAN 2000, were jointly hosted by Ghana and Nigeria. It brought together members of both the Ghana Dance Ensemble and the National Dance Company of Ghana. Core groups and several dancers, body builders, stilt walkers and masqueraders and other artists made history. The events earned much recognition for dance and the arts generally. The overwhelming success of the Ghana 2008 Africa Cup of Nations Tournament and the AfHF Hockey Africa Cup of Nations held in Ghana in 2009 largely built upon the achievements of the previous tournaments, all headed by the National Company at the National Theatre.

Africa Cup of Nations 2008

Meanwhile, many amateur dance groups in the country, influenced by Mawere-Opoku's innovative dance arrangements, were further influenced by this new dance phenomenon. A youth dance group, called Youth Absorption Programme (YAP) and later renamed Dance Factory, was formed by the National Theatre administration and modelled on the work of the National Dance Company. Even though the group did not appear to have a clear professional and artistic vision, it brought together talented young dancers who performed in their own amateur dance groups and in the Dance Factory. With the help of Adjetey Sowah the group developed a few credible dance pieces – a significant contribution to the pool. Notable among the Dance Factory's works was a choreographic treatment of the famous opera *Madam Butterfly* and a moving piece entitled *Living with AIDS*.

In the regions, many of the Centres for National Culture establishments maintained resident groups, basically specialising in their own brand of neo-traditional Ghanaian dances. At Cape Coast in the Central Region, the Agoro/CILTAD was established as a project by Nyomi Selete to help revive that city's artistic life. The project was funded by the Danish Development Agency (DANIDA), to organise young men and women in music, dance and theatre. Agoro/CILTAD did enormous work on theatre for development programmes in the region. The project successfully staged the famous South African musical, *Ipi Tombi* with a Ghanaian accent. The experience the dancers of the Agoro/CITAD gained, during its rather short life span for such a useful project, contributed in no small way to the ongoing development of dance in Ghana.

Noyam African Dance Institute

A new genre of dance, *Noyam* or *Contemporary African Dance*, is gaining currency in Ghana. The language of this dance form is universal in orientation, but its inspiration, content and symbols draw from the African experience. Contemporary African dance therefore negotiates between the old dance traditions and the impulses and issues of Africa's new generation. It redefines and distils the intrinsic values, vitality and contradictions of the African dance tradition to sketch out something uniquely African. It reasserts the art of dance in a contemporary idiom and at a higher and universal level of artistic consciousness. In a nutshell, contemporary African dance reflects the moment and the place. It is not bound to the past. Its aesthetic standard and means of expression help portray human lives, views and innovations in a contemporary context.

Noyam, which translates as 'Moving on' or 'Development' in the Ga-Damgbe language of the people of the Greater Accra Region, is a dance technique as well as the name of the institution. This technique derives its norms from the movement characteristics, aesthetic qualities and philosophy of the African dance traditions; as well as from international artistic forms and products, and from stakeholders.

This advances the notion that, as African socio-cultural and economic practices evolve, so also should its art forms reflect these changes. Contemporary African dance is being developed by choreographers and other creative people with artistic insights and technical skills. These are people exposed to local and international artistic forms and products, who have acquired a holistic outlook that informs their teaching, choreographic and technical methods.

The Noyam African Dance Institute is in the forefront of this dance phenomenon in Ghana. The establishment of the Noyam Institute – also with funding from DANIDA – came out of its founders' resolve to bring pre-university dance education to Ghana. After the 80s, the non-residential certificate course offered by the University of Ghana to prepare candidates for its diploma course was phased out. Before Noyam was established in 1998 therefore, even though dance students were being trained at the university, there was no secondary level dance institution to equip prospective entrants for its School of Performing Arts. The Noyam African Dance Institute, therefore, obtained initial approval from the Ghana Education Service, (GES) under the auspices of Ghana Ministry of Education, to operate as the first private dance institution in Ghana, in line with provisions of the Ghana Education Act of 1961.

The objectives of the institute are to provide opportunities to diverse groups of young people of varied educational backgrounds to learn about dance in innovative ways, and to provide systematic professional training for seasoned dancers. Students are taken through the theory and practice of both traditional and contemporary African dance. They help to develop new ways of creating and presenting Ghanaian dance and to change Ghanaians' perception and attitude to dance as a serious profession.

Training

Noyam derives its technique and methodology from the enormous movement and rhythmic resources available in various African communities. *Noyam* also looks at compatible elements from international artistic forms and products as well as experiences of practitioners involved in development of dance in Ghana and elsewhere. The style and vocabulary of *Noyam* are based on the philosophy that the human body is the life force, the tool for creating and disseminating dance, that mirrors people's experiences. Dance should therefore not be limited in its ability to absorb movement, wherever it comes from, so long as it reflects the true nature of its source.

Noyam dancers in a contemporary African dance   Photo Karla Hoffman

In addition to its teaching, the Noyam Institute includes the following: a group of past graduates who help with teaching and demonstration activities of the institute, and a Research and Documentation Unit, which records its activities and helps to codify traditional and contemporary African dance movements. There is also a programme for exchanges between students and teachers of the institute and other institutions, both within and outside Africa.

Using the style, vocabulary and techniques of *Noyam*, the dancer must acquire the movement skills needed for effective execution and definition of dance. To achieve this, students are taught a selection of traditional dance movements, ensuring that they learn the proper execution and details of each dance. The teacher pays particular attention to shape, dynamics and the contextual and emotional qualities of the movements. Movement improvisation is an important part of contemporary African dance; students are required to improvise on specific movements during the course. The Noyam curriculum also takes advantage of the enormous movement and rhythmic resources in traditional games such as *Nteewa*, *Ampe* and *Ntoosa*, rhythmic games for girls and boys, respectively.

Other everyday movement activities are explored for choreography. Exploration of space, even though not much emphasised, forms an essential part of contemporary African dance. Kinetic energy derived from such everyday human activities as falling, lifting, jumping over things, walking, clapping, rolling, pushing and pulling of things, running, natural undulation of the spine and facial expressions of all sorts form part of the process. Of all these resources, perhaps the observation of people in places like markets, funerals, and festivals provides the richest resources for dance creation. In addition, individual explorations by teachers and students of abstract movement feature prominently in the institute's activities. The dancing body, like any communication tool, is like a sponge that soaks up ideas from all these different sources.

It is the Noyam Institute's policy to expose its students to as many different dance techniques as possible. Teachers from varying technical, artistic and cultural backgrounds share their knowledge and experience with both faculty and students. Daily dance technique sessions, derived basically from traditional dances, are held to address this important aspect of dance training. The final decision about what materials to use as vocabulary – words, sentences and phrases for a particular dance composition – is guided by the evolving choreographic language of contemporary African dance.

Some of these dances are applied as they are, while others are abstracted, extended, stylised and filtered into the choreographic works of the institute. Enduring choreographic works like *Koom* and *Sochenda* by Nii-Yartey, and *Mirage* and *Djemba* by his former students, Okuley Tetteh and Ashai Trebi respectively, draw on these wide-ranging vocabularies to exemplify the characteristics of the Ghanaian style of contemporary African dance referred to as *'Noyam'*, while *Koom*, meaning, water, in the Dagbani language of the Dagomba people of northern Ghana, explores man's relationship to this precious element: philosophically, spiritually, and socially. The images in the piece represent some African belief systems and the attitude of some Africans to water.

Sochenda, also in the Dagbani language, means the 'traveller'. *Sochenda* speaks to situations that one may encounter in life; in particular, the trials of human experience that one may have to endure. *Mirage* depicts how as humans we all reach out to life in our own unique ways. In moments of need, however, we expect to lean on others. Sometimes, though, our expectations are illusions of what others can do for us. *Djemba*, meaning 'character' in the Ga–Damgbe language of the people of the Greater Accra Region, looks at the individual in society. The solo dancer in the piece expresses or simulates regret where he falters in his dealings with members of his community and shows jubilation when society commends his responsible behaviour.

In the years since its inception in 1998, the Noyam Institute has trained several students, many of whom are Ghanaians, while others are from South Africa, the United States, the UK, Jamaica and the Netherlands. Some of these graduates have set up their own dance companies or gone back to their mother institutions with the knowledge they gained. At least one student earned a Master's Degree in Choreography at a Dutch university, with a further from the Noyam Institute.

The requirements of the creative process and visual manifestations of its final product may vary among cultures. This notwithstanding, it is common in all human situations that every creative pursuit requires corresponding conscious physical skills, competence and a creative mind to lead the audience to an aesthetic judgement. However, the African concept of creativity and its physical manifestation includes its social purpose, symbolism and aesthetic quality, as an important part of artistic production and expression. (Paraphrasing Gyekye 1996:127)

Noyam International Dance Festival

As part of its programmes and activities, the Noyam Institute organises an International Dance Festival every two years in collaboration with other stakeholders. The festival showcases not only Noyam's works, but also achievements by other institutions, groups and individuals in neo-traditional and contemporary African dance. It provides a forum for all participants to discuss issues affecting dance and dance practitioners in Africa.

In Ghana, an annual National Festival of Arts and Culture (NAFAC) is held along with traditional festivals in many parts of the country. Hitherto, such festivals, particularly NAFAC, focused on a combined celebration of the arts. It therefore became necessary for dance artistes to create a platform for sharing ideas about African dance traditions and explore emerging forms, whilst considering how the 'old' can influence the 'new' without negating each other.

The first International Dance Festival to take place in Ghana was held in Accra from 10 to 11 December 2004. The Noyam Institute collaborated with the Institute of African Studies, and in partnership with the National Theatre of Ghana, the International Center for African Music and Dance (ICAMD); the School of Performing Arts; the University of Ghana, Legon; Fontys Dance Academy, a leading Dutch institution for dance training in Europe; Mundial Productions, another Dutch institution and one of the world's major festival organisers. PIPPA'S Health Centre and neuroGHANA, a brain and spine surgery, both based in Accra, contributed funds and facilities. Major financial support was provided by the United States Information Service (USIS), the Royal Netherlands Embassy, as well as other institutions and individuals.

The festival theme was 'African Dance – Challenges of Preservation and Development' and was aimed at students of the performing arts, community dance groups, professional dancers, choreographers, dance academics and the wider public. The festival's objectives were:

- to create a forum for dance artistes, dance practitioners and students to interact and exchange ideas
- to showcase current developments in dance
- to promote a wider public awareness and appreciation for neo traditional and contemporary African dance
- to promote artistic collaboration.

The festival also showcased neo-traditional and contemporary African dance forms such as the *Agbekor*, originally from the Volta Region of Ghana. It was performed by the Ghana Dance Ensemble of the Institute of African Studies at the University of Ghana. The National Dance Company of Ghana presented a dance-theatre piece, *Solma*. The following companies performed contemporary African dance pieces: *Tché-Tché* from Cote d'Ivoire, runners-up at the African Choreographic Competition held in Madagascar in 2002, performed *Geeme*. The Noyam Institute performed *Sochenda*; Ijodee from Nigeria, the 2004 Contemporary African Dance Champions, performed *Ori*, while Fontys Dance Academy from Tilburg, the Netherlands, presented *Chain of Collaboration* by a combined group of Ghanaian and Dutch dancers. Another combined group representing the Greater Accra regional dance groups performed a series of neo-traditional dances as a curtain-raiser.

Emeritus Professor J H Kwabena Nketia, a former director of the Institute of African Studies, discussed the role of dance in traditional communities and advised contemporary African choreographers to base their creative works in both traditional and contemporary African contexts. A two-hour dance workshop was conducted by Adedayo Liadi and the late Beatrice Kombe, artistic directors of Ijodee and Tché-Tché Dance Companies, as part of the festival. The workshop drew participants from the various dance companies and the general public.

Liadi took participants through warm-up exercises and floor work. He dwelt on body and movement isolation and ripples extracted from the dance traditions of Nigeria. Kombe, on the other hand, explored spatial elements and their relationships with the body. The enthusiastic participants interacted extremely well and the impact of the festival was profoundly felt among the artistic community and the general public.

CHAPTER 5

Creativity and Technique

Creativity and technique are perhaps the two most essential elements in the phenomenon we call dance. The two represent truth and beauty, body and mind – the tools of the trade that bring the dancer closer to a sincere physical, emotional and intellectual experience. Style, imagination, motivation, discipline and dynamics are needed in the creative process and the acquisition of technical proficiency.

In many parts of Africa, academic discourse gives scant attention to the art of dancing, due to inadequate documentation and little formal approach to creativity and a dancer's technical ability. Discussions on dance are often ethnographic and descriptive. The objective of the Noyam African Dance Institute therefore, is to bring to the fore some of the existing knowledge of creativity and technique in African dance to help broaden our knowledge on the subject.

Creativity

Creative imagination and its physical manifestation by humankind sustain the wheels of human progress and development. The creative ingenuity of the individual is, however, born of and propelled by both internal and external factors. Creativity is a phenomenon of human invention from which original ideas emanate; and which, according to Brewster is "a process of change, of development, of evolution in the organisation of subjective life, every creative act overpasses the established order in some way and in some degree". (1952)

The creative process is a challenging and sometimes painful, lonely and uncertain journey. Its expressive qualities and realisation live within the imagination's consciousness. The creative effort of the dance artiste, therefore, requires total surrender to this inner consciousness. Although it is sometimes difficult to achieve this surrender, when the artiste develops purity of motive and instinct through dedication and discipline and is informed by the depth of his or her mind, it will lead to a degree of creativity.

The African notion of creativity goes beyond the conscious level. It finds expression in both the conscious and unconscious levels. This approach, therefore, uses a creative process determined both by spontaneous procedures associated with the subconscious mind and by premeditated, conscious processes. The African learns the intricacies of dance creation in his community through social experiences and formal training. This enables the artiste to give expression to his or her emotions, feelings, and ideas in gestures and movement, forms and structures, that reflect his culture's creative processes. Thus it is essential for the creative artiste to understand the language and symbolism of dance and the community's customary behaviour before he or she can alter them on the artistic journey.

In Ghanaian communities, the creative artiste must improvise and ensure an emotional input within his or her creation's framework. He or she must avoid unnecessary exaggeration. Artistes must maintain rounded body position and relax their knees. They are expected to incorporate simultaneous use of several movement and rhythmic patterns to strengthen the relationship between the music and the movements of the dance.

The spontaneous process of the unconscious mind still requires some methodical approach; otherwise it becomes difficult to fully give form to the creative outcome. Every little bit of information and material gained through life's experiences – both mundane and the sublime – must be scrutinised. In the domain of consciousness the artiste develops personal technique, style and identity. In other words, the artiste must be able to transition from creativity to technique within the margins of what his society will allow. This spontaneous joy of creating dance requires the use of movement imagination that enables the dancer's body to internalise and express the delicate nuances of dance.

To the African dancer, acquiring this imaginative ability is what gives flight to the emotional requirements and meaning to dance. Rudolf Laban (1980) also talked about the idea of movement-thinking, as opposed to thinking in words that, "could be considered as a gathering of impressions of happenings in one's own mind, for which nomenclature is lacking. ...This thinking does not... serve orientation in the external world, but rather it perfects man's orientation in his inner world in which impulses continually surge and seek an outlet in doing acting and dancing."

To acquire the subtleties of body control, the dancer is guided by the community's dance traditions. African dance emphasises the collective representation of community as well as individual expression. It demands stamina as well as economy of movement. Movement orientation in many communities is earth-bound – in tune with gravity. Dynamic interplay among energy, gravity and resistance, for example, reveals the Ghanaian concept of weight. This concept, exemplified in the dynamic qualities of movement that society assigns to men and women, the old and the young, the king and the ordinary citizen, dictates how the dancer in each category should perform. In the *Adowa* dance of the Ashanti for example, the dancer creates calculated shapes and poses in consonance with the accompanying music, using the torso, head, arms, hands, legs and feet to make both symbolic and aesthetic statements, understood and appreciated by his community.

When a Ghanaian king dances, he is playing a role of the father of the people, the spiritual leader as well as the military head of the community. These roles require of him a thorough knowledge of the emotional and dramatic qualities – grace, dignity and strength appropriate to his status and the community. He must understand the behavioural patterns associated with his office: perform the different movements, gestures, and understand the musical accompaniments of the various royal dance forms, as well as their contexts of performance. He therefore goes through almost a life-long study of the combined techniques of delivery in all these disciplines before becoming a king. As a military leader, the quality of his movements must be strong and sharp as he takes deliberate and calculated steps forward. He assumes his fatherly position through alternate throwing of the arms back and forth in a controlled fashion. At the end of the sequence, with open arms, he thrusts both arms towards his chest.

As the spiritual head, the king's countenance is more reflective and solemn; his movements are less strong. However, the ordinary citizens dance with vigour and abandon, while the female dancers show femininity through soft and subtle movements. This is so because each dance plays a specific role in the community. Thus in the *Dipo* puberty women's dance of the Ga-Damgbe in the Greater Accra Region, the initiates must be subtle in their movement. Gentle flicking movements of the hands and smooth and unhurried shuffling steps, combined with a slight diagonal tilt of the body, are the basics of the *Dipo*. The role of music in the creative process is extremely important to the African. Nketia (1965) notes that, "when the beats of the drums die down, usually the dancing also ceases. Hence, the dancer and the drummer work in close collaboration in creating and re-creating orderly sequences of sound and action."

Mawere-Opoku (1987) confirms the above observation when he writes: "The impetus coming from the musical ensemble is the propulsive power which initially moves one to dance. It is the rhythmic percussive structure and organisation of tones, pitches, and timbre of the drums which characterise a particular dance... The dancer needs to be roused... or organised emotionally and physically, and creatively stimulated through successive musical stages." This interrelatedness informs the creator's practice and learning of dance in the community. In the *Akom* of the Ashanti of southern Ghana, the *atumpan* drums, played with two curved sticks, dictate the basic steps of the dance, while the *twenesin*, played with the hand, provides intermediary movements and creates the psychological rhythmic patterns to help induce possession in the priestesses.

Technique

Technique is the ability of the individual to perform his or her activities efficiently. The need for a good body and mind technique to help give voice to the creative imagination of the dance artiste cannot be over emphasised. Grieg (1994) aptly expresses this need when she writes: "There can be no substitute for the experience of moving in a finely tuned instrument through space, with mind and body in subtle harmony... To the African dancer however, a finely tuned body may not necessarily be a slim and athletic physique. Rather, it is the kind of body that has the ability to respond to the subtleties, as well as the energy, required by the movement and musical complexities of African dance – whether it is a big or small, tall or short, young or old, male or female body.

African dance technique goes beyond the physical ability to control and manage movements. It is integrative and combines dance with music, drama, poetry, costumes and, in some cases, masks. This is especially evident during the traditional festivals which bring people together to renew community experiences. On such occasions the dancer's body is the vehicle through which he or she communicates the movement ideas, symbolic meanings, aesthetic values and ideals of the people. Generally, African dance avoids movement that extends the body beyond what it normally does. The dancer obeys the requirements of the particular dance form and his body's capabilities. Each dance maintains a certain measure of technique within its structure, producing the overall quality of dance technique. Thus in the *Dea* dance of the Frafra of Ghana, the dancer performs simple but powerful stamping movements on the ground. He steps with the right foot on the strong beat of the music while his left takes a short light step forward on the weak beat. The body tilts slightly to the right as he repeats the stamps on the right foot and sways to the left on the weak.

The details of this dance contrast with the technical requirements of another dance, the *Bima* also of the Frafra. The *Bima* dance uses alternate and multiple, strong and forceful movement combinations of the feet. The arms, held in front of the body, perform thrusting movements from the shoulder area, while the torso tilts forward slightly. This dance's technique hinges on the quality of foot-stamps and the thrusting movements of the shoulders. However, in the *Sebre* dance of the Dagarte people, multiple chest movements in a contract-and-release fashion form the basis of technique for the dance. The *Bamaaya* dance of the *Dagomba* similarly uses rotating hip movements as the technical basis of the dance.

In sharp contrast to the techniques required in the above dances, subtlety of movement forms the basis of technique in Akan dances. For example, according to Muware-Opoku (1987), the distinguishing characteristics of Ashanti dances like the *Adowa* and *Kete* are the intricate and subtle manipulations of hands, arms and legs; body sways and tilts in polyrhythmic combination – expressive miming with rich symbolic undertones and body control.

In addition to the acquisition of specific dance techniques, special recreational activities such as the *Nteewa* hand clapping and *Ampe* multi-rhythmic games for girls, and *Djama*, a rhythmic game-of-strength for men, instil rhythmic sense, movement discipline and trust in the dancer from an early age. According to Mawere-Opoku, "the ability to express oneself competently and to communicate ideas, emotions, and knowledge through the language of dance is recognised as an important attribute of a cultured, educated citizen." Mawere-Opoku notes that "...the training of the dancer lasts throughout the dancer's lifetime. A sense of rhythm and timing are taught through voice simulations of drumming with hand clapping, miming to work chants, and the recitation of dramatic incidents in folk tales at storytelling sessions. This sustained training programme makes it possible for a dancer to meet several dance situations, even the most technically demanding." (Muware-Opoku 1987:194).

In discussing technique, we also look at new developments in African dance that reflect the socio-cultural realities of Africa today; at the same time we are examining the relevance and acceptability of new dance ideas which embody values of the African creative philosophy. In addition to the preservation of traditional dance, many African choreographers have undertaken studies (so far made internationally) of the mechanics and anatomy of human movement to advance various dance techniques in Africa.

CHAPTER 6

Challenge for the Creative Artiste

The creative artiste seeks to extend the vocabulary of African dance and push the spatial, stylistic, creative and technical boundaries beyond their present limitations. He or she aspires to formalise and codify the results of the people's creative energies, inspired by criteria and processes largely accepted in the artistic world. To deal with creativity and technique requires the African creative artiste to look at the wide-ranging and integrated training programmes available on the African continent and elsewhere, to develop viable, three-dimensional, unlimited artistic products.

Dance addresses fundamental issues of human experience and existence. To paraphrase Tracy Snipe: ...we dance to express our physical, psychological and spiritual state of being that enables us to give meaning and context to our greatest joys, hopes, frustrations, fears or sorrows. This expression contributes to a sense of wholeness... This statement resonates with the African concept of a total dance experience. To the African creative artiste, a sense of wholeness occurs when creativity and technique conspire to produce the creative consciousness needed for a meaningful dance experience.

Nii-Yartey's Personal Creative Vision

As a principal advocate of Ghana's new concept for African dance, my creative vision and challenge are to ensure a good marriage between my personal experiences and my culture. My artistic life came out of my background as a royal born and bred in a crowded area of Bukom in Accra. Bukom provided an environment full of activity, colour and excitement.

I was immersed in such activities as children's games, music, dance and rituals, as well as traditional group fighting competitions and, of course, boxing (which incidentally has produced a number of world champions from the area). I could have become a boxer or something else. These experiences have helped shape my artistic thinking in many respects.

My formal choreographic career began under the tutelage of the late Emeritus Professor Albert Mawere-Opoku, the founding artistic director and choreographer of the Ghana Dance Ensemble. My strong traditional background, studies – both in Ghana and abroad – and exposure to dance during my world travels profoundly helped shape my creative vision. I succeeded Mawere-Opoku as the artistic director and choreographer of the Ghana Dance Ensemble in 1976, a position I left in 1993 in order to found the National Dance Company at the newly established National Theatre of Ghana.

From my perspective as a choreographer living in Africa, I have drawn on a spectrum of creative impulses based on my experiences and perceptions of the world. I begin by creating a safe world in which I get lost allowing my imagination to float in different directions. Strange as it may sound, in many cases, I am able to operate simultaneously on both the conscious and unconscious levels. Every so often I drift off into my creative mode, especially when involved in a production. Sometimes this leads to random thoughts of moving images and ideas of unknown origin. At the same time I am conscious of activities in my surroundings. My response to stimuli and these spontaneous ideas gradually merge to become snippets of artistic interests with which I build an artistic product. Often this process is full of restlessness and anxiety.

In many situations, I feel as if I have internalised the opposing forces of my conscious and unconscious mind: being an African on one hand, while acknowledging the influences from my experiences outside Africa on the other. This conflict sometimes lingers until I reach what I call the core factor. The core factor is a segment of an idea so concrete, so clear, that the movements, the dance, the staging and the lighting, all crystallise. I integrate as many core factors as I can generate, until they are not core factors so much as the embodiment of the production. I sketch out composite images of body posture, props, floor patterns etc. It is only then that I begin to apply the elements of space, style, dynamics, levels, and other details of dance creation. I also pull much from the collaborative efforts of dancers, musicians and lighting and scenic designers to give form to the final dance I create.

As director of the National Dance Company of Ghana, my involvement in one-on-one, choreographer-to-choreographer co-productions offered me the privilege to work with some of the most creative, crazy and kind artistes from other cultures. They included Louise Akin of Cote d' Ivoire, Jean-François Duroure from France, Monty Thompson from Trinidad/the US Virgin Islands, Germaine Acogny from Senegal, Nana Nilsson from Sweden/Denmark and 'H' Patten from UK/Jamaica, Bob Ramdhanie from Trinidad/UK and others. I discovered from them and others' collaborations that the creative process always requires a paradigm shift.

Egos and uninformed perceptions can obstruct the artistic process. It is always difficult initially when one deals with the other person's preferences, perspectives and cultural nuances. However, when both artistes discover common ground everybody begins to relax. Each progressively learns to accept the qualities the other brings to the process. Both finish the collaboration richer than when they began. What I have learned during my many years of involvement in co-productions living and sharing with people of different cultures is that the more exposed one is to other cultures the easier one can deal with the problems associated with such complex artistic collaborations.

The Creative Process

Here is a look at the making of the historical dance-theatre: *Musu – Saga of the Slaves*. The production script was written by F Nii-Yartey. Material for the creation of *Musu* was researched by Irene Korkoi Odotei, F Nii-Yartey, Olaf Henson, Sidsle Jacobsen and Monty Thompson. *Musu* combined, for the first time, major poetry by Kofi Anyidoho and music composed by Nana Danso Abiam, two of the best in these areas. Costumes were designed by Grace Djabatey, stage-sets and props by David Amoo, and stage lighting by George Kartey.

Three countries were involved: Ghana, Denmark and the US Virgin Islands. Two choreographers from Ghana and Trinidad/US Virgin Islands put the pieces together. Two major dance companies – the National Dance Company of Ghana and the Caribbean Dance Company performed at the main event in Copenhagen, where *Musu – Saga of the Slaves* was the flagship production of that city when it became Europe's cultural capital in 1996. The use and combination of the various artistic forms were approached with all the tools of the production team – their vision, experiences, artistic capabilities and maturity, as well as trust and teamwork, and the generosity and commitment of the production's funders, the Danish Development Agency (DANIDA).

Before embarking on the production, we asked ourselves several questions. For instance, how do we treat a subject like slavery from three different perspectives in countries where slavery is hardly discussed without touching on sensitive issues or contradicting ourselves and history? More important, how do we faithfully treat such a serious historical subject in a dance-theatre where there is little or no dialogue to help advance the story? How do we stage facts of history that don't easily lend themselves to artistic treatment? How do we reconcile the artistic sensibilities, egos and the cultural backgrounds of all the different creative partners in a way that positively enhances the production?

To answer these questions, we brainstormed with tact, self-restraint and, above all, mutual respect. We discussed the main events and characters and the roles they played in the various incidents, particularly during the period of Danish involvement in slavery in Ghana, Denmark and the now US Virgin Islands. We agreed on, or sometimes allowed, our research findings to determine the direction to go – in spite of our

Left and below: Merging different perspectives

Above and right: Perceived roles

personal interpretations of various events and how they related to our perceptions and attitudes to slavery.

However, in the process, we took a lot of artistic liberties. For instance, Aquando, an Akwamu king between 1600 and 1725, was described as a wicked king who killed many of his own people and sold them into slavery, and was himself killed in battle by the Ashanti. He fits perfectly into the role of betrayer of the African cause, and therefore became a symbol of betrayal in the production. King June, who probably ruled between 1725 and 1773 as a king of the Akwamu, reportedly was captured during battle with the Ashanti and sold to the Danes as a slave in the month of June; hence the name King June. He was described as "a remarkable man whose temper, surprising firmness and authority", making him our obvious choice for hero and king in the production.

The character of Queen Mary in history organised the burning of

Frederiksberg on the Island of St. Croix. She was our Yaa Asantewa of Ashanti and our heroine. Sadam Akim and Adum were Akwamu citizens who in the 1800s were arrested by the Danes for sacrificing two young girls to a set of *Fontomfrom* drums. They were sent to a Copenhagen prison and are depicted in our artistic interpretation in the production as innocent people who were practicing their faith. Governor Philip Gardelin, described as a "colourless and efficient" administrator who promulgated some of the worst laws against slaves in the Virgin Islands, became the villain and the embodiment of a terrible slave master in the production. In addition, we created a visual representation of some of the situations or actions which precipitated the capture of many Africans into slavery.

For example, even though the Africans did not historically declare full-scale war on the Danes, the latter interfered in the spiritual and other affairs of the Africans. In the production, therefore, King June declares war against the Danes for arresting Sadam Akim and Adum. The selfish and inhuman behaviour of the slave masters as they scramble for gold, ivory and slaves and pillage and rape the local women are captured in scene Act 2 Scene 3. A slave merchant, chasing a slave girl to rape her, instigates a fight among his peers, resulting in the slave girl freeing King June and other condemned prisoners, thus saving them from execution. We brought the characters in the production together, regardless of when each one actually lived, to help tell our story.

Mapping the stage

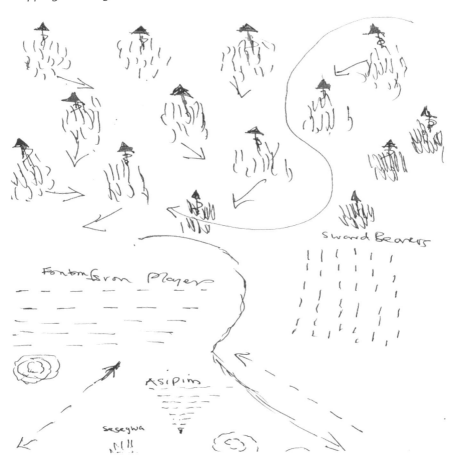

CHAPTER 7

Safeguarding Ghana's Cultural Future

I have attempted to offer a basis for the construction of at least a semblance of the history of dance development in Ghana since its independence in 1957. I have also tried to discuss the characteristics, significance and practice of dance and establish the context within which traditional forms and the emerging contemporary genre operate in both traditional and contemporary situations, and the events that influenced the changes in dance over the past decades. These events include the achievements, failures and conflicts of the period and the institutions that served as catalysts in shaping the direction of a National Theatre Movement in Ghana.

Traditional dance still enjoys patronage almost everywhere in Ghana. However, since 1962 professional dance has become a serious part of Ghana's development agenda, as it is in most countries. Ghanaians with Master's and PhD degrees in dance, choreographers, dance teachers, administrators and dancers of international standing now share recognition with other professionals. Many of them teach or perform all over the world. Obviously, this is a great achievement by third world standards; it needs to be sustained and taken to greater heights.

However, in a country where so far, funding for the arts has been almost non-existent for many years, the promise partly realised by the achievements of the past several years hangs precariously. The National Theatre Movement has been unduly stalled; ignorance, apathy and the inclination to deny the arts their rightful place in the priority of government programmes threaten the existence of the arts in Ghana.

Dance is an important art form in Ghanaian culture. I believe that the government of Ghana should recognise, as did the Fourth Republican Constitution of 1992: "Culture as a necessary tool for national integration and development" with the realisation ... "of the vision of the people of Ghana to respect, preserve, harness and use their cultural heritage and resources to develop a united, vibrant and prosperous national community with a distinctive African identity and personality and collective confidence and pride of place among the comity of Nations." (National Commission on Culture 2004:1) Immediate steps must be taken to make the study of dance – traditional, neo-traditional and contemporary – in all our schools a required part of Ghana's education system.

It is also my hope that appropriate government agencies, as well as civil society, will support and fund well-focused and sustained dance education programmes, festivals, workshops and conferences in the spirit of the constitution and the cultural policy of our country. This will help ensure that Ghanaians do not lose this important aspect of their culture and that future generations embrace the important role dance plays in their social, physical, spiritual and economic lives.

Above: "Even though most traditional African dances are abstract in a larger sense, there is always some kind of story – either personal or based on community experience" (Kwabena Nketia) Photo by Karla Hoffman

Right: Neo-traditional version of the Adzogo Dance

A dance-theatre by F Nii-Yartey Photo by Karla Hoffman

Noyam, which translates as 'moving on' or 'development' in the Ga-Damgbe language, is a dance technique as well as the name of the Noyam African Dance Institute

Noyam Dancers in the Spirit of Dance Photo by Karla Hoffman

Solma by F Nii Yartey Photo by F Nii-Yartey

Above: Images of Conflict by Nii-Yartey and Germaine Acogny   Photo by Karla Hoffman

Left: Francis Nii-Yartey

CHAPTER 8

Selected Productions

The presentations of the following choreographic pieces show the efforts made so far to build on what has already been achieved in dance development in Ghana since Independence. They also demonstrate attempts being made to script some of these choreographic works, with varying degrees of success, to help capture some essence of these works. Unlike plays and musical compositions, choreography or dance compositions cannot boast scripts or scores to guide their creative processes and the finished products. I hope, when fully developed, it will be of great interest and benefit to students of dance and professionals who wish to document their creative works, as well as non-professional readers who want to add to their knowledge of dance.

With the exception of the *African Liberation Dance Suite* by Mawere-Opoku, I wrote, choreographed and directed the greater part of the following works, some of which I co-directed and co-choreographed. They range from purely stage presentations to special events like mass outdoor presentations.

The list is arranged in a chronological order of works.

African Liberation Dance Suite (1965)

Story and Choreography: A Mawere-Opoku
Music: Members of the Ghana Dance Ensemble, Legon
Lighting: Paul Aliba
Costumes: Margaret Agyeman

Exploitation and Enslavement of the Sleeping Giant Africa

The dancers use appropriate arduous working movements of *Lobi* songs with xylophone and percussion accompaniment to illustrate forced labour, unending toil and tired limbs.

The Awakening, Restlessness, Agitation and Call to Arms

Here, the Asafo war dancers dance around the standard-bearer and the leaders, who arouse the tired workers to agitate and fight for their rights. Their womenfolk join them to cheer them on into battle. Sounds of heavy fire send the crowd off into the wings of the stage.

Lamentation for the Dead and Dying Freedom Fighters

- *Husaso* – a Yeve cult theme introduces the anxiety of the people and rumours of massacres and mass arrests of dead and dying fighters. Funeral dirges and songs of lamentation follow
- *The Atsea* – a gay dance used to reassure the living that though dead, the late comrades will continue to fight alongside as an invisible powerful spiritual host; hence the rejoicing
- *Husago Theme* – but alas! We shall miss their physical presence, their counsels and warm embraces.

The Struggle for Freedom Shall Continue till Victory is Won

We shall fight on with unabated vigour and determination in the face of expected reverses and sacrifices, and then we shall lay down our swords and rejoice. The *Anlo Agbekor War Dance* fittingly expresses the theme of the finale to this suite.

The Lost Warrior (1978)

Story and Choreography: F. Nii-Yartey
Costumes: Margaret Agyeman

The Lost Warrior is dance-drama, which was inspired by the *African Liberation Dance Suite*, and portrays the invasion of a village, Anlotovi – disturbing the peace and tranquillity enjoyed by the people.

As a result, the men take up arms to defend the village. Anlotovi is victorious. Unfortunately, however, one of the warriors loses his life. As custom demands, the community mourns his death before victory is celebrated.

Ghana Dance Ensemble in 'Lamentation for Freedom Fighters' by Mawere-Opoku Photos: Joseph Pietterson

The King's Dilemma (1979)

Story and Choreography: F Nii-Yartey
Costumes: Grace Djabatey
Set Design: David Amoo
Music: Traditional Music
Lighting: Emmanuel Quartey

Nyindongopio, the King of Nyindongo, is in a dilemma. An unassuming young stranger and the king's chief bodyguard are each claiming the honour due for having killed a wild beast that has for some time been terrorising the people in the peaceful Northern Ghanaian town of Nyindongo.

A confrontation between the chief guard and the stranger establishes that the latter is the true killer of the beast. The town, therefore, accepts him as a citizen of high position. This infuriates the disgraced bodyguard. To wipe out his shame, and seeking vengeance for his defeat, he steals the

king's crown, symbol of power and authority, and plants it on the stranger in a cunning and deceptive manner that convinces almost everybody present that the stranger is indeed the culprit.

However, one of the town's progressive female leaders has cause to suspect the bodyguard. She convinces the other women of the stranger's innocence. However, the shocked and rather perplexed king, in his confusion, banishes the stranger from the town. To see that justice is done, the women stage a political coup, and remove the king from power.

Bukom (1986)

"The crowd loved it. This is what theatre for development is all about." Weekly Spectator, Ghana

Story and Choreography: F. Nii-Yartey
Costumes: Grace Djabatey
Set Design: Roy Mettle Nunoo and David Amoo

Juvenile delinquency usually erupts from broken homes because of unfavourable social conditions. Amartey comes from one such home. As a result, he falls under the hypnotic influence of the area gang the

'Bukom Champs.' However, an unfortunate event – which takes place during one of the gang's anti-social activities and results in the death of his mother – opens a new and positive page in Amartey's life. He decides to take on the responsibility of helping the other gang members change the course of their lives as well. First, they must wait for the opportunity to get rid of the notorious and charismatic leader of the gang in any way possible.

Photos: F Nii-Yartey

African Dance in Ghana: Contemporary Transformations

Akwankwaa (1985)

Story: Kwabame Okai
Choreography: F. Nii-Yartey
Costumes: Grace Djabatey
Set Design: David Amoo

Akwankwaa is based on a song of the same title by the late Ghanaian musician Kwabame Okai. The piece portrays how a young woman gambles her life away in the hands of death through overindulgence in money matters. *Akwankwaa* cautions about vice and worldly things and reminds us of the inevitability of death.

Atamga (1989)

Story and Choreography: F Nii-Yartey
Costumes: Grace Djabatey
Set Design: David Amoo

The people of Havevi have sworn the greatest oath of the land, *Atamga*. For three days in the month of November that very year, they will observe a communal worship in honour of their god Dzidegbe. During this period, they will abstain from all carnal acts and keep themselves pure or face the wrath of Dzidegbe.

The community, however, fails to honour this social and religious obligation because an unknown evil force has taken over the minds and spirits of the entire population. This spell compels community members to commit some of the most atrocious crimes their society has ever known.

Dzidegbe, therefore, embarks on the destruction of the people because they disobeyed him. Fortunately, Akowe, the chief priest of the community, convinces Dzidegbe through appropriate rituals and prayer that the people's unacceptable behaviour was caused by a force bigger than the community.

To protect the community against the evil force and to forestall a future reoccurrence, Dzidegbe gives them one of his virgin and spiritually strong daughters to protect them. She unexpectedly falls under the spell of the evil force and becomes an incarnate of all that is evil. To overcome the evil force, Dzidegbe must destroy his own daughter.

The Legend of Okoryoo (1991)

"The audience went away at curtain call with a lot of them having had a good initiation into what dance production is, or should be." Nana Banyin Dadson, The Mirror, Ghana

Story and Choreography: F Nii-Yartey
Costumes: Grace Djabatey

Set Design: David Amoo
Musical Effects: William Anku
Performers: Members of the Ghana Dance Ensemble

The central theme of *The Legend of Okoryoo* is man's ingratitude and greed.

The Oleetei, makers of life, conceive Okoryoo, the epitome of a perfect woman and a messenger of peace. She emerges from an egg. Her first divine mission is to hatch a giant egg within a specific time from which will emerge other celestial messengers who together will bring peace, love and prosperity to the human race.

Failing to hatch the egg after a prolonged attempt, Okoryoo sets out to Earth to accomplish what should have been a collective task. In her encounters with the human race, they crave material prosperity to the exclusion of peace and love. However, Okoryoo soon runs out of her bounty.

This inflames the greedy passions of the human race whose members, in their rage, sentence Okoryoo to the gallows. Meanwhile, the giant egg has hatched and the other celestial messengers, not finding Okoryoo, set out to fulfil the Oleetei bidding as initially ordained.

Photo: F Nii-Yartey

The celestial messengers reach Earth in time to save Okoryoo from the gallows. They use their celestial powers to subdue the human race. Then to fulfil their original divine mission, all the celestial beings, together with the human race, fade out into one of the eggs. The egg will hatch in another millennium, after which they will emerge as one entity with one soul and purpose in fulfilment of the divine will of peace, love and prosperity.

Nkulunkuku (1993)

"...A perfect piece which has tremendous relevance to mankind." Weekly Spectator, Ghana

Choreography: F Nii-Yartey
Costumes: Grace Djabatey
Lighting: George Kartey
Set and prop design: David Amoo

The shroud of Jesus may not necessarily be the only item that contains his powers. As a carpenter's son, one would have expected that Jesus must have manufactured a few items in his father's shop. Such items of a great man must contain some of the powers he exhibited during his lifetime and after.

In the creative imagination of the choreographer, Jesus made many items, including a stool while working with His earthly father, Joseph. In this dance piece, this stool somehow finds its way to Ghana.

The Christians in the country discover the powers of the stool through a vision. However, many take these powers for granted. This situation changes when a prophet begins using the powers of the stool to cure various afflictions.

Obaapa (1995)

Concept: Female Musicians in Ghana
Story and Choreography: F Nii-Yartey
Music: Helena Rabbles
Costume: Grace Djabatey
Stage props: David Amoo

Obaapa (the ideal woman) is a modern rendition of the *Dipo* puberty dance for girls of the Ga-Damgbe people of Ghana. The piece, which combines movements from the *Kpatsa* and *Takai* dances of the same people as well as movements from the modern dance of the youth, was to honour the former First Lady of the Republic of Ghana, Mrs Konadu Agyeman-Rawlings. It expresses the beauty and dignity of the modern African woman.

In the piece, under the protection and inducement of their leader, young initiates learn the intricacies of womanhood and the joy of being role models for the future.

The men effectively provide the necessary support and exhortation for their womenfolk.

The National Dance Company of Ghana in 'Obaapa' by F Nii-Yartey
Photos: Opare 'Blowman'

African Dance in Ghana: Contemporary Transformations

Musu – Saga of the Slaves (1996)

"A tight plot with revealing sub-plots build up to a shattering climax that leaves one totally drained. It is as if all the energy Nii and the performers expend in the process of giving us Musu *is what they take out of their audience in replacement."*
Enimil Ashong, Weekly Spectator, Ghana

Story: F Nii-Yartey
Co-choreographed by: F Nii-Yartey and Monty Thompson
Director: F Nii-Yartey
Costumes: Grace Djabatey
Set Design: David Amoo
Music: Nana Danso Abiam and the Ghana Dance Ensemble.

Musu – Saga of the Slaves, seeks to explain the nature of some aspects of the slave trade. It is something that should not have happened. Musu, meaning an abomination in the Ga and Akan languages of Ghana, is inspired by incidents that occurred during the Danish slave trade from about 1672 to the 1800s and the choreographers' own interpretation, as artists, of events and personalities whose feats of courage and defiance are chronicled in historical accounts of the period.

This production also attempts to provoke humankind to reflect on the whole issue of slavery worldwide. In the treatment of materials on the subject, the choreographers took a few artistic liberties to help them achieve aesthetic and other artistic credibility. Several factors contributed to the making of *Musu- Saga of the Slaves.*

Prologue
Slavery is a dent on our conscience – frozen images of our painful past. The poet talks for us. A poem, specially written and performed by Kofi Anyidoho, opens the performance, as he interacts with the frozen dancers with burning torches on stage.

Act 1: Scene 1 – *The Gold Coast (In the Community)*

The highest priests of a Ghanaian community are on their way to a secret grove to perform rituals ushering in the New Year. The lesser priests and priestesses, who dance to awaken the populace and remind them of the coming event, follow.

Ablavi, a character representing the young ladies in the community, has awakened early today and witnesses the tail end of this rare phenomenon. She calls out her peers for household chores in anticipation of the celebration. The local flutists announce the commencement of the event. The king of the community enters in grand style. Those invited from neighbouring communities arrive with messages of goodwill. The usual displays and exchanges of artistic ideas and other manifestations abound.

The chief of Akwamu, Nana Akwando, arrives with his two daughters to give a message of solidarity from his people. His arrival, however, does not please Adum, son of the chief of Nkotunse, who is Nana Akwando's arch rival. A timely intervention by the king, however, saves the situation. The community receives Akwando's message with

enthusiasm as they all join in the celebration with heightened zeal. A strange sight interrupts the celebration! The white man has arrived! After initial surprise and suspicion, they establish a measure of trust between them – the uninvited visitors and the ever-friendly Africans. Mission statements made; welcome gestures exchanged.

Act 1: Scene 2 – *At the Christiansburg Castle – Osu*
According to the spiritual powers he has inherited, Sadam Akim, the spiritual leader of the community, must sacrifice two virgins to the *Fontomfrom* drums, symbol of the community's spirituality, to avert the reoccurrence of what has befallen them. The Danes, however, arrive to arrest Akim and charge him with murder before the ritual is completed.

Act 2: Scene 1
The king declares war on the Danes for depriving the community of their spiritual leader. The Africans have almost won the battle; however, Akwando, whose two daughters were the virgins Sadam Akim sacrificed, joins forces with the Danes and betrays the king and his people. The Danes capture the king. The whole community is in turmoil. One of the slave merchants falls in love with a young slave woman.

Act 3: Scene 1
In the dungeon, the slaves go through mental and physical agony. They struggle to free themselves, but to no avail.

Act 3: Scene 2
The ships finally arrive. The slaves go through a tunnel into the bowels of the waiting ships. The slave merchant is still pursuing the young woman he's fallen in love with. The slaves raise the alarm! They capture and molest the merchant. All the slaves scatter and struggle to free themselves when a colleague of the merchant shoots and kills one of them. The slaves manage to swim back to shore. Akwando, however, betrays them. The slaves lament on their way back into captivity and are shipped to the Danish West Indies (US Virgin Islands).

Act 4: Scene 1 – *The Danish West Indies*
In the Danish West Indies, various people buy the slaves. A rich happy-go-lucky merchant, J R Soedtman, buys King June, who becomes chief butler at Soedtman's reception parties. After one such party and after one glass too many, King June recalls who he was back in the Gold Coast.

Act 4: Scene 2
The slaves till the land and plant sugarcane and cotton on the island. In the meantime, the atrocities continue. The slave masters foil many rebellions planned by the slaves.

Act 4: Scene 3
The slaves demand freedom and Governor Scholten, the islands' chief administrator, grants it. However, it does not take the 'free' slaves long to realise that the freedom gained is not real, for nothing has changed. They are still enslaved.

Act 4: Scene 4

More forced work and little in return. The resultant mob action leaves a white overseer dead. The slaves face various forms of punishment, including death.

Act 4: Scene 5

The slave merchant is still pursuing the young woman. His colleagues follow to see what he does with the girl. A fight erupts among them. In the process, the young slave woman frees King June and the others.

Act 5: Scene 1

'Queen Mary', one of the strongest and most widely respected women among the slave population on the island of St. Croix, decides to mobilise the other women to burn the property of the white population.

Act 6: Scene 1

On the Island of St John there is drought and very little to eat. King June is not happy. He organises his supporters against the slave masters. The slaves kill many of the whites and share their property. King June and his men decide to take over the island. Some of the blacks betray their cause to the whites. For six months the rebels fight but they run out of ammunition and other essential supplies. Still they fight on. Finally, the Danes call in French soldiers from Martinique to help quell the rebellion.

Tired and hungry, King June and his compatriots realise they are completely surrounded – but to die at the hands of the people who have enslaved them for all these years will not be a dignified death. Suicide is the answer!

Act 6: Scene 2

As the slaves lie dead, smoke fills the stage, creating a misty atmosphere. One by one the dancers rise from mist to the dictates of the poet. They walk slowly in a calculated fashion towards downstage as they look straight into the eyes of the members of the audience. The lights fade into darkness and come back on to reveal the dancers still looking. This is repeated a few more times.

The Epilogue

The end has come. Slavery has officially 'ended'. However, after slavery, how is the African faring? The poet sums it up as the dancers move slowly toward the audience, looking into the future through the voice of the poet.

Note on the curtain call for this production

This ending is meant to unsettle the members of the audience and to get them to reflect on the subject. There are instances, where this approach to a curtain call, caused the audience become openly fidgety, and many of them literally leave the theatre unceremoniously.

Solma (1995)

"Solma is intelligent, moving and spectacular; it is performed with controlled elegance at the same time producing a dynamic almost feverish spectacle." The Guardian, London, October 9, 1995

"This dazzling company lets you know immediately how truly wonderful African dance can be...All the arts were here but triumphant dancing carried the day and stays in the memory." Richard Edmonds, The Birmingham Post, October 25, 1995

Story: F Nii-Yartey and Jean-Francois Duroure
Choreography: F Nii-Yartey and Jean-Francois Duroure
Costumes: Grace Djabatey
Director: F Nii-Yartey
Music: The Ghana Dance Ensemble

Solma, meaning 'to tell a story', is the result of a meeting between the creativity and richness of the dance forms inherent in the African

traditions and an exploration of contemporary dance ideas. This climaxes in fireworks of rhythms, colours, movements and sounds that go beyond the message which *Solma* seeks to convey. *Solma* is also about contemporary Africa.

The trials and tribulations of urbanisation; the colours of the theatre and the sounds of the vibrant market places; love, lust, jealousies and gang life; political aspirations and solidarity in the face of oppression; and, ultimately, traditional African spirituality and cultural resilience: all are explored in this fast-moving dance within the context of today.

Sal-Yeda (1998)

"...choreography was exceptional; – its movements were expressive and actually came from the soul" FLASH, Ghana

Story and Choreography: F Nii-Yartey
Costumes: Grace Djabatey
Set and Props Design: David Amoo
Music: Angelique Kidjo and Mariella Bertheas

Humankind's insatiable desire to have control over the Earth results in reducing him to a situation of wretchedness and to a desperate need for survival. To survive, therefore, man must seek the intervention of 'Asaase Yaa', custodian of the Earth, to help rejuvenate him and his environment. However, this intervention requires a process of confusion, hunger, prayer, conflict, pain and finally death – as a form of cleansing.

Images of Conflict (1999)

Story: F Nii-Yartey
Choreography: F Nii-Yartey and Germaine Acogny
Lighting: Chris Duplech and George Kartey
Set and Prop Design: David Amoo
Costumes Design: Grace Djabatey and Claire Kan
Sculptural Design: Kofi Setordji
Musical Arrangement: William Anku

The term 'conflict' in this production is an all-embracing one. The choreographers explore both positive and negative sides of conflict. Water and fire, for instance, give both life and death, the two are constantly in conflict.

The dancers perform various movements to indicate activities of the cosmos. Soon, they begin to develop various emotions. They love and hate. Later, their emotions intertwine. The dancers gather in a circle around a glow of fire performing different but coordinated movements to suggest Unity in Diversity. Four other people appear in shadows, holding modern torchlights. They perform various movements. Some of their relatives in the circle, however, become suspicious and attempt to stop those who want to get out of the group. Conflict ensues among the dancers. Those who want to follow the torches eventually are able to do so.

Water suddenly extinguishes the fire in the center, as the dancers perform toward different directions. Their movements suggest conflicts and the subsequent breakup of the unity. Various sculptural images depicting the effects of conflict are in the background. Resolution occurs when dialogue and consensus, through the performance of similar movements, takes place between the various factions, resulting in the re-lighting of the fire.

Everybody dances joyously, intertwining beautifully with the 'torches' in coordinated movements. Sounds of water form the background as the dancers perform harmoniously in solos, duets and in small spiralling groups, forming a spiral of life. From the spiral, they all move into a circle with the sound of water trailing behind the dimming lights.

Images of Conflict, choreographed by F Nii-Yartey and Germaine Acogny

African Dance in Ghana: Contemporary Transformations

Fire of Koom (1999)

"The Fire of Koom showed a Ghanaian dance troupe at its contemporary best." Enimil Ashong, Weekly Spectator, November 10-16, 2001

"This is a post-modern dance. This is what I refer to as the honesty of the artiste. This artiste has been honest with his art. He [Nii Yartey] has taken what other cultures offer and truthfully and honestly blended the two." Judith Jamison, Alvin Ailey Dance Theatre, Weekly Spectator, Ghana. September 28, 2002

Story and Choreography: F Nii-Yartey
Costumes: Grace Djabatey
Set Design: David Amoo

Fire of Koom ('Koom' means 'water' in the Dagbani language of the Dagomba people of Northern Ghana) was inspired by issues concerning water and degradation of the environment in some parts of Accra and its environs. We made several visits to these areas to observe the problems associated with water shortage. We discovered that the people usually pray, quietly, hoping that things will correct themselves.

On the other hand, they curse, rave and point fingers at the water

company and city authorities for not doing their work well, while they themselves do nothing about the situation. *Fire of Koom* is an example of the role the arts play in raising awareness about one's civic responsibilities. A work of art like this provides a mirror for society to come to terms with itself and compels it to change for the better.

Left: the author dancing with Judith Jamison, Artistic Director of Alvin Ailey American Dance-Theatre, when the latter was installed as an honorary Queen Mother of a division of the Ga People of Ghana

Sochenda (1999)

*"It will take a lot of time to absorb what has gone into me these past few days in Ghana. With that queen mother enstoolment ceremony, those two dances (*Fire of Koom *and* Sochenda*) and the speech by that learned Professor (J H Kwabena Nketia). I need time to absorb."* Judith Jamison, Alvin Ailey Dance –Theatre, Weekly Spectator, Ghana

Story and Choreography: F Nii-Yartey
Composer: Souleymane Koly
Costumes: F Nii-Yartey

Sochenda, meaning 'traveller', is a philosophical journey of man as a traveller in this world. The piece speaks to the situations that one may encounter in life; in particular, the trials one may endure through the human experience, including the inevitability of pain and death.

Sochenda performed by Noyam

The Power Within (2003)

Story and Choreography: 'H' Patten and F Nii-Yartey
Costume: Grace Djabatey
Se and Props: David Amoo
Lighting: George Kartey.
Sound: Tahiru Mohammed and Nii-Tete Yartey
Stage Assistant: Kofi Ahiavor

Some leaders are born; others become leaders. Society sometimes bestows power on leaders. Some steal it, while others think its acquisition depends on one's social standing. However, real power lies within its owner. *The Power Within* is a dance-theatre piece which depicts a struggle for power between Saprewa, a man endowed with leadership qualities of spiritual proportions and Wobli, a pathological usurper who must have all power and control possible. Unfortunately, the majority of the community seem to favour the usurper, because of their ignorance of who Wobli really is. However, this situation does not last long! Who will have the real power to turn things around to uplift the people? Who will have the last say?

Asipim (2002)

"Asipim is as much dance as it is drama. The story-line, the plot characterisation, representation– all the elements are at play here, including judicious use of space, and above all, tension... This was a gripping performance by a team which understands each other. This Nii-Amoo-Grace combination is an exportable commodity." Enimil Ashong, The Spectator, February 2002

"There was no point in time that the set was left bare, it was all action till the very last bit of the curtain call." Jayne Bucnor-Owoo, Graphic Showbiz, February 27, 2002.

Story and Director: F Nii-Yartey
Choreography: F Nii-Yartey and C K Ladzekpo
Collaborators: Sano Kemoko and Malonga Casquelourd
Costumes: Grace Djabatey
Poetry: Kofi Anyidoho
Set and Props: David Amoo
Lighting: George Kartey

This is a story about the quest for and misuse of power. It is also about greed and gallantry, and supernatural powers. It is about pageantry and peace, political power...it is of madness and of love. Above all, it is about the power of Dance (*Statement by F. Nii-Yartey*).

ACT 1: Scene 1 – *Road to the Throne*
Map of Africa is formed by the cast upstage. Sound effects of thunder; horns and lightning; background song 'Africa', sung by the cast, dominates the other musical effects.

Ataa Din enters from stage right as if coming from inside 'Africa'. He performs selected movements from the *Agbekor* war dance as he surveys the entire stage. Downstage left is a special golden throne of Africa. He approaches the throne. Agor, his rival, enters from the opposite direction to stop Ataa Din in his tracks.

A fight ensues, developing into a fierce spiritual encounter over the throne. Ataa Din is defeated but just as Agor is about to give the coup de grace, Awo Din enters. She is in an advanced stage of pregnancy.

Awo Din pleads with Agor to spare her husband's life. Agor attempts to take over an amulet, which has fallen from Ataa Din's neck during the fight. Awo Din manages to take her fatally wounded husband to safety. Agor fails to get hold of the amulet because its powers are too much to contain. Awo Din and Ataa Din exit. Agor follows disappointedly.

Wise old man enters. He shares a few words of wisdom with Africans. He notices the amulet and picks it up, turns to the audience and smiles. He exits. Suddenly, the map of 'Africa' bursts open with colours and vigour. The cast scatter all over stage, holding pieces of the Africa map – some running or somersaulting, others jumping and creating general excitement. They merge to perform the *Agbekor* dance.

Awo Din enters in a distressed mood. She announces the death of her husband to the community, which mourns with her as they sit in a large circle, clapping and singing. The town crier enters with a consolation song for the mourners. Awo Din is in labour. An elderly woman seeks the help of the men to lift her up. The singing heightens. A baby cries... and finally, a baby boy is born! Some members of the gathering present various gifts to the baby. Awo Din presents her amulet to the baby. The anxiety turns into excitement.

Awo Din shouts – a second baby is coming! The town crier continues dancing and encouraging Awo Din. He performs the naming ceremony for the twins. The wise old man presents the amulet to the second child. The mother receives the babies. The gathering goes into frenzy. A group of women admirers usher Awo Din off stage. All exit with her.

ACT 2: Scene 1 – *The Enthronement*
An attendant carrying a huge metal bowl is led on to the stage by the chief priest of Africa. The attendant places the bowl at center stage. Three other attendants enter with Agor. The chief priest orders Agor to cleanse himself ritually in the bowl, in preparation for his installation as king of Africa. Agor takes a few calculated steps towards the bowl and does running steps around the bowl. He performs a few arm movements, ending with a sudden stretch of the right leg above the bowl. He enters it and cleanses himself. He exits with the priest. Two other attendants join the three on stage. They place the bowl on the head of one of them, making spiral movements towards up stage left. The carrier remains up stage left with the bowl. The others leave to take their positions upstage center. The chief priest enters with Agor. He beckons the latter to stop, and orders two attendants carrying royal paraphernalia on to the stage.

ACT 3: Scene 2 – *Celebration of Power*
Agor is installed as king. Four *Takai* dancers who enter stage right and left join him. The new king is ushered onto the throne. The palace of Africa is set in a dimly lit background, as sections of the main set are pushed into position.

Celebrations begin. Eight women enter from stage right and left to pay homage. They perform a *Guinean* dance. Eight male dancers enter to perform the male version of the same dance. The dancers form a circle and the men and women take position alternately in the center of the circle. The men finally form a ring, holding hands in the middle. The women sit on the men's arms and kick their legs. The circle moves counter-clockwise into a file. The women drop from the men at a cue from the drummers, and each group forms a straight line towards the opposite direction – stage left and right respectively. They exit. Two Jembe drummers enter to play for the king.

Four more Guinean dancers follow them. Congolese dancers take over. Arrangements of the *Gota* dance follow. Oko and Ate perform a dance. Ate does a solo, bringing an added excitement to the celebration with his extraordinary dance routine.

ACT 4: Scene 2 – *The Challenge*

In the process, Princess Teteele joins in the dance with Ate, by the end of which she completely falls in love with him. The gathering hails Ate for his extraordinary dance feat.

However, to King Agor, hailing and raising Ate above him constitutes an act of treason, much more so since Ate has seduced his daughter. The king descends his throne and charges at Ate. Awo Din pleads with the king not to hurt her son. Agor insists he must teach Ate a lesson. He notices the amulet around Ate's neck and grabs it! Ate pushes the king away from him. The soldiers save the king from falling backwards. Agor pushes Ate down and orders his arrest.

In the meantime, Teteele is going through excruciating mental agony over Ate's arrest. She pleads with her father on Ate's behalf but without success. Agor pauses for a moment to admire Awo Din. Awo Din is not interested. The entire population is shocked and confused over the whole incident. Everybody starts to leave the durbar grounds, in twos and threes.

The king casts a spell on Awo Din as she leaves the palace with some of the women. The men also leave, while three of the women decide to attend to the princess, who by this time is completely unhinged. Teteele shouts hysterically and acts in such an outrageous and unbecoming manner that the three women are afraid to touch her. Her shouts draw the king's attention. Teteele will not allow him to touch her, running around as her father chases her.

Awo Din is completely under the spell of the king. Oko does not know what to do as his mother heads towards the king. Oko notices the

strange behaviour of Awo Din as
he confronts the all-powerful
King Agor. Oko charges at him.
The king responds fiercely, using
his spiritual powers. Oko cannot
withstand the powers of Agor,
and runs for his life.

Several weeks later Teteele
is seen completely insane and in
tatters. She confronts the wise
old man and chases him away.
King Agor summons the chief
priest to provide a cure for his
daughter but the chief priest
cannot. Teteele escapes from the
shrine. A spiritualist transfers the spiritual powers from Ate's amulet to
the king. The amulet is finally in the hands of King Agor. Ate now is
powerless. The king banishes him from the town.

ACT 5: Scene 3 – *The Marriage of Awo Din*

Several people appear on a half-lit stage holding pieces of cloth to drive
away evil spirits before His Majesty's marriage to Awo Din. Four of the
dancers spread their cloths on the floor. The people exit. Twelve young
women enter in groups of threes. Each places a calabash on the cloth
alternately. When they are all set, the twelve young ladies begin to play
Nmani music.

Four columns suddenly drop from the roof on to the stage amidst
thunderous and powerful music, as part of the setting of the scene. Men
and women enter the stage, busily mounting various other settings and
generally preparing for the wedding. Several men enter to purify the
place by snapping pieces of cloth around the stage. A group of people
usher in the king and his bride-to-be. The dancers performed the
following dances in succession: *Tora, Jira, Atsea, Congolese* and *Guinean*
dances.

Close to the end of the wedding Oko arrives on the scene to attack Agor. The King sensing danger casts a spell on all the supporters of Oko to neutralise them. A fight ensues between Oko and the king. The king overpowers Oko and orders his arrest and summary execution. The women plead with the king to spare Oko's life. The king pays no heed. The women are upset and confront the King.

Suddenly, Teteele appears on the scene, causing pandemonium and destroying everything she can find. She mistakes Oko, the identical twin brother, for her lover, Ate. She runs after him, leaving behind a chaotic situation in the palace. The women begin to clean the mess and the men join them.

King Agor, highly impressed with what the women have done, relents. Realising the extent of damage his fears and greed have caused him, his daughter and indeed, the people of Africa, he reverses his position and orders Ate from exile. He pardons Oko and revokes the love spell on Awo Din. Teteele embraces Ate. The spiritual effect of the reunion restores Teteele's sanity.

The community finds that King Agor is guilty for murdering Ataa Din and for his cruelty to his own subjects. He hands over power to Oko. The chief priest enters with a group of women carrying pots of dried leaves. They symbolically bury Agor by pouring the leaves over his head to bury his shame and to signify the end of his reign as King of Africa. To bury his shame, the king runs and jumps on a web of ropes hanging from the roof of the stage from which he struggles as the light fades.

AfHF Hockey Africa Cup for Nations, Ghana 2009 – Opening and Closing Ceremonies Choreography

Story: F Nii-Yartey
Executive Producers: Ministry of Youth and Sports; Ghana 2009 Hockey Local Organising Committee (LOC); and Magnus Rex Danquah
Production Team: Noyam African Dance Institute
Event Director and Choreographer: F Nii-Yartey
Administrator and Finance Director: Korkor Amerteifio

Music Composer: William Anku
Casting and Logistics Director: Martin Owusu
Research and Documentation: Oh! Nii Kwei Sowah
Event Coordinator: Terry Bright Ofosu
Set and Props: David Amoo
Costume Designers and Wardrobe: Grace Djabatey-Laing and Fabiola Nyarku

Opening ceremony – *The Prologue*

To achieve the ultimate in sport, we need to unite as Africans on our common dreams and aspirations – as well as the vast human and natural resources available on the continent – as we interact with the rest of the world in the various fields of sport. The unity of purpose and determination with which our countries conduct their business in all sporting activities, therefore, will go a long way in evoking the blessings and gift of success from Mother Africa.

The birth of field hockey on the African continent only adds to the knowledge that, as a people, we have the capacity to excel in all fields of sports if we share and strengthen our resources and support each other as a family. In the end we will have cause to celebrate our achievements, not as individual nations, but as a unified Africa. That is the way it is meant to be and that is the way it should be. So let's begin to dream again!

Story: Uniting the future

A flag-bearing Ghanaian messenger travels across the continent, extending Mother Africa's invitation to all her children to converge on Accra to participate in the continental hockey tournament. The family celebrates the gathering with special traditional dances: *Atsea*, *Adzobgo*, *Sohu*, *Agbekor*, *Sikyi*, *Wongo*, and *Nagla*. The celebration ends in the formation of the fihankra symbol – the Adinkra symbol of unity.

Gift of Africa

All welcome the appearance of Mother Africa with good prospects, circumstance and expectations, as a group of *Sokodei* dancers evoke the spirit of fertility; and prepare for Mother Africa's arrival in Accra. She brings along with her the spirits of Nigeria, Ghana, Egypt and South Africa; and not least, pomp, pageantry and a sense of achievement.

The birth of field hockey

For the first time in the history of the continent, Father Africa joins his wife and children. In the meantime, he is challenged by forces seeking to prevent Africa from achieving its goals. However, through his resilience and resolve, Father Africa finally succeeds in supporting Mother Africa in giving the gift of African hockey!

The game

The first real hockey is played and the winner declared. Thereafter, led by Mother and Father Africa, members of the clan disperse to their various locations in the continent.

Sequence of events

1   A solitary Ghanaian flag-bearer runs diagonally across the pitch and in different directions.
2   Other Ghanaian flag-bearers join in from various points searching for other Africans. They break into smaller groups and head in different directions.
3   Flag-bearers of Egypt, Nigeria, Kenya and South Africa emerge from the directions the Ghanaians are heading towards.
4   All flag-bearers merge to perform *The Africa Dance* made up of movements from cultures of participating countries including the *Asafo* dance.
5   More dancers join the flag-bearers to form an 'Adinkra' symbol of unity at the center of the pitch.
6   *Tonto* dancers dressed in white, enter to perform various stylised movements.
7   The *Adinkra* and *Tonto* dancers come together to perform various traditional dances and movements. They exit in different directions after the dance.

8   A group of *Atsea* dancers – each holding a large handkerchief in each hand – enter, overlapping the exit of the previous group.

9   They spread across the pitch to perform various movements of the dance.

10   A loud atmospheric sound ushers in Mother Africa carried aloft; and richly dressed special *Dipo* costumes. A large shiny piece of cloth (boi), trails behind her. (A group of hockey players are hidden under the boi.) A number of people carry skeletal frame of umbrellas and skeletal sections of a huge egg.

11   Mother Africa and her entourage make their way to the centre. As she gets closer, the logo begins to pulsate and expand – opening up for her to enter. The boi is wrapped around the hockey players to form a semblance of an egg; as the logo group exits in various formations.

12   Various *Ogede* dancers make up groups of fours, eights, etc. that overlap as they enter from various sections of the pitch and perform towards the egg after going through various dance routines.

13   A male dancer walking on stilts and dressed in a majestic costume enters to perform some acrobatic routines. Accompanied by special sound effects, he makes a gesture towards the egg.

14   The egg bursts open, releasing the hockey players who are seen busily playing a serious game as the rest of the cast slowly exits.

15   The hockey players form groups of three, each assuming the position as depicted on the lower section of the tournament logo.

16   They break off on the sound of the referee's whistle. They make friendly gestures toward each other as they exit.

17   A large number of musicians and dancers enter in a celebratory mood. They are accompanied by other performers holding long silvery poles, symbols, and more silvery skeletal frame of umbrellas. They perform various dance and other artistic routines.

18   The entire group dances to the center of the pitch to form the logo of the tournament.

19   The National Anthem of Ghana is played.

Closing ceremony – *The End Statement*

So soon, the game is over – the gathering of the clan has achieved its objectives. It's time to reflect on the achievements of the tournament. We are all winners, so let us celebrate! Even if victory tonight belongs to only one country, the joy goes to all of us... so let's begin to dream again towards the next competition as we honour our deserving heroes and heroines with the *Kete* royal dance and the celebratory music of *Damba*.

Sequence of events

1 *Kete* and *Damba* dancers and musicians provide the heartbeat of the game.
2 The future is represented by a group of *Tonto* girls.
3 Symbols of fair play and unity guide the seventeen special trophies of the tournament.
4 The ushering in of the symbol of life, the giant egg – signifying the continuous life and growth of the game of hockey on the African continent.
5 Finale: the spirit of Africa soars upwards into the heavens to inspire the people and to spread the positive outcome of the tournament across the world.

The closing ceremony

African Dance in Ghana: Contemporary Transformations

Glossary

Movement action: an idea behind a movement being performed

Movement quality: the quality or definition of movement of the body

Movement awareness: mental and physical connection that helps to propel a particular movement

Kinetic experience: ability and awareness of mobility in the body

Rhythmic impetus: basis for regular pulse in music or dance

Dramatic action: required moments of intense action in dance performance

Melodic: pertaining to a pleasing musical quality

Percussion: quality of movement denoting a striking action

Linear: relating to dance formations or direction of dancer in lines

Multi-linear: a dance performed in several linear formations

Regulative beat: main controlling pulse of music or dance

Phrase: a sequence of movements forming a section in dance

Misago or **Husago:** an Ewe expression meaning 'tie the pot'. It is also a section of a religious dance of the same people

Movement aspects of customary behaviour: movements associated with everyday activities, such as pounding, greetings and hunting, etc.

Movement complex: multifaceted movements usually associated with a particular dance form

Abstract: a form of extracted dance or movement, usually with an elusive meaning

Performance ability: skill and craft needed to be acquired for dance performance

Durational rations: length of time apportioned to sections of a dance

Labanotation: a system of dance notation developed by German dancer and theorist, Rudolf Laban

Contraction: in dance, the constriction of the muscles of the body

Cyclorama: in the theatre, it is a large curtain or wall dividing up-stage and back-stage

Core factor: a term denoting the epitome of artistic material needed for dance creation

Yaa Asantewaa: a heroine in Ghanaian history who led the male fighters of Ashanti to fight the British Colonial powers in 1900 to protect the Golden Stool, the embodiment of the soul of the Ashanti people

Durbar: a gathering of the community, usually in the presence of the king to deliberate on national issues or during the many annual traditional festivals held in Ghana

Nmani: a musical form in which the womenfolk play large calabashes accompanied by songs.

Afterword

In November 2015, while attending the Africa-India summit in New Delhi, F Nii-Yartey died unexpectedly. His friend and colleague, **David Amoo** – former Artistic Director, The Ghana Dance Ensemble, National Theatre, Accra – remembers Nii-Yartey:

"I worked closely with Nii-Yartey, Grace Djabatey, Addokwei Moffat and George Kartey as crew for the National Dance Company of Ghana and the Ghana Dance Ensemble for more than three and a half decades. My relationship with Nii sprang from our days at the Institute of African Studies, University of Ghana campus, in Accra.

"During the early 1980s, I was engaged in traditional dance and music performances under Nii's directorship at the National Dance Company of Ghana. Nii had taken over that position from Professor Albert Mawere-Opoku, the father of neo-traditional dance. Nii saw what I had done in designing and constructing sets for many dance productions staged by the University of Ghana's School of Performing Arts; he asked me to stage manage the National Dance Company in Accra at the National Theatre in 1992.

"At the National Theatre, Nii engaged his troupe in an experimental transformation aimed at restructuring Ghanaian traditional dances to fit contemporary contexts. He was interested in seeing indigenous dances developed as an internationally acclaimed dance genre. Nii infused indigenous traditional dances into his choreography, paying strict attention to selection of movement, clarity of movement execution, and spirited performances from the dancers.

"For decades the National Dance Company of Ghana/Ghana Dance Ensemble earned fame and respect across Africa and the world at large, serving as a cultural ambassador and attraction for foreign visitors. As Nii developed dozens of theatrical dance productions, I worked with him designing and constructing sets, providing "reference and perspective", as one critic reported, that "transported the audience back into time and culture". My scenic creations were inspired by indigenous African symbols that were relevant to what we aimed to achieve on stage.

"Nii and I were in complete agreement about how to employ set design and construction materials to realise his theatrical dance productions. Our relationship as colleagues became a friendship that was as close as that of two brothers; an unseen chemistry of two minds at work with a shared vision.

"After Nii retired as Artistic Director of the National Theatre in 2006, I took over his position. Nii then became Head of the University of Ghana Dance Studies Department at the School of Performing Arts, where I also joined him as a part-time lecturer in design.

"It was with great sadness that I learnt of Nii's death in December 2015, while in India carrying out an assignment for the Institute of African Studies. I love and will greatly miss my brother."

Entering Nii's world

Marian Horowitz had the privilege of working with F Nii-Yartey for several months in 2013 to edit this book. Here she remembers her time working with Nii:

"Nii recognised that, although an amateur dance enthusiast, I had little understanding of African dance and certainly no experience with Nii's fusion of indigenous Ghanaian dance into a contemporary version of Ghanaian dance. But such was Nii's passion for dance, his enthusiasm for sharing that passion, and his ability to communicate and teach about dance, that the hours we spent with his manuscript became a joyous labour of love on both our parts. Nii embraced the idea of relating clearly and economically the history of Ghanaian dance and his own role in developing international appreciation for both traditional Ghanaian dance and his contemporary interpretation and restructuring of that dance tradition. Yet he was adamant that we retain the flavour of the dances he described—their movements and emotions.

"In the same way that Nii's photographs of his dancers enabled David Amoo to create illustrations that captured the feeling and movement of the dance, Nii used his own body to show me what he meant by dancing 'into the ground', or how to use one's arms to express a spirited yet subtle emotion. He would beat out for me (on any available surface) the rhythm which accompanied certain movements. In this way he drew me into the spirit, technique and passion of his dances, so that together we could describe them with precision and feeling.

"Nii-Yartey had a great love for life and a great love for advancing the traditions of Ghanaian dance. He wished for the whole world to experience it, appreciate it, and allow it to enrich the lives of everyone who saw it. I believe that Nii's love for life infused his choreography to make it the vibrant, exuberant, yet controlled experience each dance is. I hope that this book will spread the legacy of Nii's immense contributions to African dance and Ghanaian dance in particular. It provides an insider's guide into a rich and complex little-known world of culture, history, and movement. Every person who reads this book will have the privilege of learning about Nii's world and consequently will learn about the man himself; every person will be the richer for it."

Professor Francis Nii-Yartey posthumously received the Millennium Excellence Award for Arts, Tradition & Culture on December 11th, 2015. An award presented to "Ghanaians who have selflessly devoted their time, effort and knowledge to the socio-economic and political development of the country" (http://mefafrica.org/mea/millennium-excellence-awards/#).

About the illustrations in this book

The illustrations for this book by David Amoo, were conceived to honestly represent the book's content, including body positions, movements, a variety of dances and costumes and, in some cases, the position of more than one dancer. A list was developed of the dances and positions from the manuscript's text. Different dances, movements and gestures, costumes, musical instruments, stage props and other distinguishing details were identified. Photographs were located from which sketches were to be developed from the portfolio library of the National Dance Company, at the National Theatre in Accra. Additional photographs were taken when no archived photograph could be located. Most of the original photographs were enlarged sizes and sufficiently large to be suitable for tracing.

In order to faithfully trace the photographs, to create sketches, clean plain paper sheets were placed over the photographs and secured with masking tape. In a dark room the paper and photographs were set onto a glass plate and backlit. The images were traced carefully to keep important details. Each illustration was inked after the sketches were traced from the backlit photographs. Photocopies were taken and either reduced or enlarged to conform to the space provided by Nii-Yartey throughout the text.

A Tribute to Nii-Yartey by his Children

In times of loss, especially the loss of a loved one, we are reminded to have faith in God's ultimate plan and in all things, give thanks. Yet how do we do this when the inspiration for our faith has gone?

We became used to your routine of goodbyes – you would select clothes to be ironed, have your bags packed, throw a scarf around your neck, and put on the waist bag that we all found amusing. You would then remind us to keep the doors locked at all times and the house clean.

You were many things to us and taught us many things, but above all, you were a disciplinarian. We heard people say many times, "e sane wa ei" ("he is difficult"). To us, however, you were strong and steady. Through you, we learned the important life lesson of causality. We will never forget your anecdote about life being like a cup, and how what you pour in your cup is what you will have to show at the end.

We remember our excitement when you would say, "Nyɛ ya jua nyɛhe, wɔ miiya Trade Fair" ("go and take a shower, we are going to Trade Fair"). We didn't mind the soap in our hair from half-done showers or the fights over who sat in the front seat because we knew you were going to sing aloud old Ga songs as we giggled in amusement.

We have never been scared of venturing into the world and making our mark. At the time when our brother Nii-Tete was torn between two important career choices, you helped him realise that there was no such thing as an easy road, and what he needed was the discipline to find the tools and the wisdom to apply them appropriately.

Our elder brother, Dr. Franklin Nii Amankwah Yartey, would speak of how challenging life had been for him, alone in the United States, but how he always found clarity and balance after talking to you.

When Nii-Tete and Nii Kwei-pe fell ill as children and were admitted to Legon hospital, you were so worried that you carried the family TV and VCR to the hospital and set up an entertainment corner, not only for Tete and Kwei, but for the whole ward – patients, nurses, and doctors.

Many of you remember our father for his love of tea, how he would wake up and brew a range of hot beverages in the morning for everyone who entered the house: for our friends, for mechanics, even for the waakye (rice and beans) seller who provided food to the Noyam dancers.

You once said to our sister Aisha: "It doesn't matter what career you want to pursue in life; you have to do it to the best of your ability to stand out. Think like a Yartey."

The most intriguing part of your story was never written. Instead, it lives on in the lives of many artists like David Amoo, Oh! Nii Kwei Sowah, Grace Djabatey, Adjetey Sowah, Jeannine Osayande, Joshua Trebi, Benjamin Obido, Bernard Woma and countless others, who will continue sharing the knowledge you gave them. You are not ordinary if you encountered Nii-Yartey because he instilled in you the extraordinary.

In life, we start off as children to our parents; when we are older, we become friends. Knowing our Father was a never-ending journey. We are embodiments of Prof F Nii-Yartey.

Though you have departed to join our great ancestors, you live on in us. Daddy, we want you to know we will continue the great work you did on this earth.

We love you, Dad, may your soul rest in perfect peace.

Bibliography

Adinku, Ofotsu (2004) *Cultural Education in Ghana: a Case Study of Dance Development in the University System,* Dance Chronicle, Vol.27, No.1, pp. 49-66, ibid. 49

Butterworth, Jo and Wildschut, Liesbeth *Contemporary Choreography, a Critical Reader (2009),* London and New York: Routledge

Gyeke, Kwame, (1996), *African Cultural Values: An Introduction,* Sankofa Publishing Company, Philadelphia, Pa. and Accra, Ghana, pp 127–128

Kwakwa P A (1994) *Dance and African Woman,* in SAGE, Vol. VIII, No.2, fall, pp. 11–12

Nii-Yartey F (2009) *Principles of African Choreography: Some Perspectives from Ghana. Contemporary Choreography: A Critical Reader,* Edit: Jo Butterworth and Liesbeth Wildschut, Routledge, Taylor and Francis Group, pp. 254–268

Nketia J H K (1965) *Drumming in Akan Communities of Ghana,* Nelson and Sons, U.K., pp.163

Nketia, Kwabena, J H, (1988) *Ghana – Music, Dance and Drama – Review of the Performing Arts of Ghana,* Information Services Department Press, Accra, Ghana

Nketia, J H Kwabena, (1970). *The Creative Arts and the Community: Proceedings of the Academy of Arts and Sciences,* Vol. VIII. Accra, Ghana, pp. 71-76

Nketia, J H Kwabena (1966) *Significance of Traditional African Music, Institute of African Studies,* University of Ghana, Legon, p. 22

Nketia, Kwabena J H (1970) *The Creative Arts and the Community: Proceedings of the Academy of Arts and Sciences,* VOL. VIII, Accra, Ghana, p. 71.

Nketia, Kwabena J H (1965). *The Interrelations of African Music and Dance,* Separatum, Studia Musicologica Tomus, V11. fasc., 1-4, p. 9

Nkrumah, Kwame (1963) *The African Genius,* Speech delivered at the Official Opening of Institute of African Studies, University of Ghana, 25th October, pp. 13–17

Opoku-Mawere A (1987) *Ashanti Dance Art and the Court, Schildkrout: Studies of Ashanti*, Anthropological Papers American Museum of Natural History, Vol. 65Pp.194

Opoku A M (1966) *Choreography and the African Dance,* Research Review Vol. 3 No1, Legon – Accra: Institute of African Studies, pp. 53–59

Opoku, M A *African Dance Perspective – Review of Basic Concepts*, Unpublished Manuscript, Institute of African Studies, University of Ghana, Legon, Ghana, pp.80

Snipe, Tracy D (1998) *African Dance: Bridges to Humanity*, African Dance, edit. Kariamu Welsh Asante, Africa World press, Inc. New Jersey, USA, pp.64

Sutherland Efua T (2000). *The Second Phase of the National Theatre Movement in Ghana*, Fontomfrom: Contemporary Ghanaian Literature, Theatre and Film, ed. Kofi Anyidoho and James Gibbs (Matatu 21-22; Amsterdam & Atlanta GA: Editions Rodopi, pp. 45 – 57

Tierou, Alphonse (1989: 1992) *Doople: The Eternal Law of African Dance*, Harwood Academic Publishers, Switzerland, pp. 18 – 19

Thompson, Farris Robert, (1983) *Flash of Spirit –African and Afro-American Art & Philosophy*, Vintage Books, A Division of Random House, New York, pp. xiii

Welsh Asante, Kariamu (1998) *Zimbabwean Dance Aesthetic: Senses, Canons, and Characteristics*, African Dance: An Artistic, Historical and Philosophical Inquiry, Ed. Kariamu Welsh Asante, African World Press, Inc. New Jersey, USA, p. 207

Name Index

Subject Index

National
    Art and Craft Gallery 22
    Commission on Culture 23,
      58
    cultural policy vi, viii
    Dance Company (of Ghana)
      iv, 32–5, 41, 50–1, 52, 97, 100
    Dance Theatre v
    Festival of Arts and Culture 40
    Symphony Orchestra 22, 31
    Theatre v, 22–3, 31–5, 40, 50,
      97–8, 100
    Theatre Movement viii, 21,
      31, 57
neo-traditional dance 23–4, 26,
    32, 41, 58
neuroGHANA 41
Nkulunkuku 68–9
Nmani music 89, 96
Noyam xi, 39
    African Dance Institute 35–
      41, 43, *Plates B–C*
    International Dance Festival
      40–1
Nteewa hand clapping 13, 38
Ntoosa 38
Nzema 1
Obaapa 69
Obonu royal dance 7, 12,
Ogede dancers 93
Ori 41
Osagyefo Players viii, 23
Otufo puberty dance 19
Pioneer Tobacco Company 29–30

PIPPA's Health Centre 41
puberty dance 19, 46, 69
religious dance 7–8, 19, 95
rhythm 5, 12–4, 44, 48
Sal-Yeda 78–9
School
    of Performing Arts 24, 36, 40,
      97–8
    of Music, Dance and Drama
      ix, 24
Sebre dance 12, 16, 47
Sikyi dance 91
slavery 21, 53–6, 71–6
Sochenda 39, 41, 83
Sohu dance 91
Sokodei dancers 91–2
Solma 33, 41, 77–8, *Plates C*
Takai dance 16, 69, 87
Tché-Tché 41–2
The Africa Dance 92
The King's Dilemma 27, 62–3
The Legend of Okoryoo 27, 33,
    66–7
The Lost Warrior 27, 60
The Power Within 33, 84
Tonto dancers 92, 94
Tora dance 89
University of Ghana v, 2, 22–4,
    27, 31–2, 36, 40–1, 97–8
US Virgin Islands 51–3, 55, 73
Wongo dance 91
Workers' Brigade 23
Young Pioneer Movement 23
Youth Absorption Programme 35